FOREST BOOKS

THE THIRST OF THE SALT MOUNTAIN

Marin Sorescu was born in the village of
Bulzeşti, county of Dolj, the fifth child of a
family of peasants. He attended secondary
schools in Craiova and Predeal, graduating
from Iaşi University with a B.A. in Philology.
Since 1978 he has been working as editor-in-
chief of the literary review 'Ramuri'.

His first volume of poetry SINGUR PRINTRE
POEŢI (Alone amongst Poets) appeared in
1964, followed by numerous volumes of
poetry, prose and drama.

His first play, JONAH, was published in
1968, followed by THE VERGER in 1970, and
THE MATRIX in 1973. In 1974, the three were
included as a trilogy in THE THIRST OF THE
SALT MOUNTAIN.

His work has been translated into most
languages, and his plays performed through-
out the world.

In 1974 he was awarded the prize for
drama by the Writers' Union of Romania
and in 1978 the international prize Le Muze
by the Academia delle Muze, Florence. In
1983 he was made a correspondent member
of the "Mallarmé" Academy in Paris and in
December of the same year he received the
International Poetry Prize "Fernando Riello"
in Madrid.

THE THIRST
OF THE
SALT MOUNTAIN

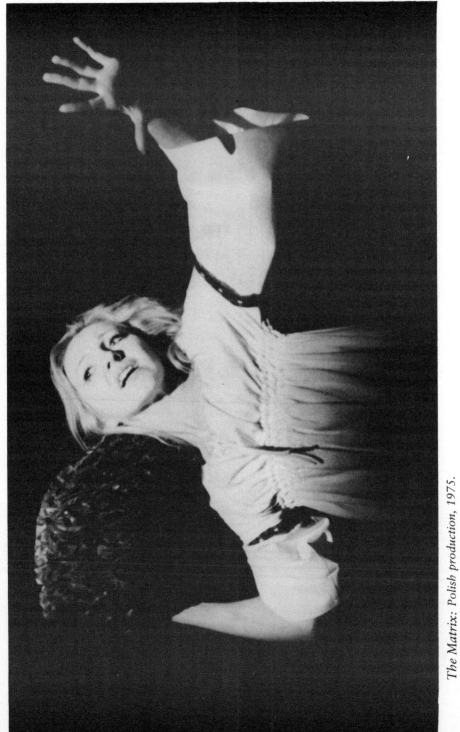

The Matrix: Polish production, 1975.

THE THIRST
OF THE
SALT MOUNTAIN

a trilogy of plays
by
MARIN
SORESCU

translated

by

ANDREA DELETANT
and
BRENDA WALKER

FOREST BOOKS
LONDON * BOSTON

Published by FOREST BOOKS
20 Forest View, Chingford, London E4 7AY, U.K.
61 Lincoln Road, Wayland, MA. 01788, U.S.A.

First published 1985

Reprinted 1990

Typeset in Great Britain by Cover to Cover, Cambridge
Printed in Great Britain by BPCC Wheatons Ltd., Exeter

Jacket design © Ann Evans
Translations © Andrea Deletant, Brenda Walker

British Library Cataloguing in Publication Data
Sorescu, Marin
The thirst of the salt mountain.
I. Sorescu, Marin. Jonah   II. Sorescu, Marin. Verger
III. Sorescu, Marin. Matrix
IV. Title. English
859'.234   PC840.29.074
ISBN 0-9509487-5-6

Library of Congress Catalog Card Number
85-070248

Contents

Something Like a Preface

I've just noticed that quite a number of years have passed since I wrote the trilogy, THE THIRST OF THE SALT MOUNTAIN. It is about an immense abstract thirst, and a rather more concrete salt mountain, situated, according to the needs of the stage, in any part of the globe. It's about something else as well, a lonely man, haunted by an immense thirst, a man who forever tries to climb this never-ending mountain of salt, stubbornly, stumbling at every step, while the mountain urges him to 'Climb! Climb! Come on, try again! Because if you don't exist, nothing has any meaning. Neither your – smaller – thirst, nor my – larger – one!'

Since then each of these plays have rolled through the world in their own way, some with more luck than others. *Habent sua fata libelli.* It's true, not even tragedies are exempt from their own destiny! JONAH travelled the most, bottled in his whale. And so I came to realize that the earth was covered three quarters by water . . .

The play which is probably closest to me is THE VERGER. In the absence of crowds from the past, the Verger lights candles in a deserted cathedral to age it. In the meantime, however, the candles have become very expensive and the need to find a new source of energy has emptied cathedrals even more. People function less and less with pure spirit, holiness now belonging, as in ancient times, to the realm of wilderness. This doesn't stop the Verger from climbing the walls in search of himself or from being exasperated by the deaf watchman, who continually removes the scaffolding. He descends into himself, then climbs towards godliness, as if 'nothing had happened'. Who knows, perhaps nothing has happened.

THE VERGER hasn't had very much luck, although when it appeared, the Romanian theatre director Liviu Ciulei was enthusiastic. (I would like to give praise, if only in parenthesis, to the excellent school of Romanian theatre, directors and actors, great on any stage of the world and who deserve to have plays written for them). Ciulei had decided both to stage and act it himself, at the Bulandra Theatre. The danger for the Verger was in falling, God forbid, from his high abstract scaffolding into mysticism. Such fears did exist. This experienced man of the theatre, the creator in Bucharest of some outstanding performances (I accept full responsibility for the use of this word), had taken all safety precautions, talking about some sort of safety belt, which would have kept the direct ascent of the character towards self-knowledge. The plan failed, as often happens in the theatre, and the play dropped from my mind, since I was completely absorbed by the completion of the last part of the trilogy.

I have tried in these monodramas to ask myself a few 'searching' questions without pretending to know the answers. Searching on the horizontal: Jonah in the belly of the biblical whale, which sways and collapses together with seas and oceans, swallowing and vomiting each other. Searching on the vertical: the Verger, a sort of anonymous and shy God, a God 'without full knowledge of the case'. But as the earth is not just horizontal or vertical but round, a womb, just as round as that of the young Irina (a character in the third play), would seem to suggest a radical and – why not say it – supreme solution to these anxieties, by the simple fact of giving birth, of bringing a child into the world at the exact moment when the world is least prepared to receive it: during the deluge, a new deluge, unacknowledged, but nevertheless disastrous. Cyclical, unquenched anxieties, spasms of loneliness in the world and in the cosmos, the attempt to transcend the human condition, or maybe only to achieve a better understanding of it.

Each play aroused great interest. At any rate, interest about my expectations. I thought I was writing for a sole spectator, myself; some personal notes connected to everyday doubts and stumblings with the sunset and sunrise, the seasons and the moment. A great deal has been written about these plays. Recently a Romanian critic was talking about 'inner paradise', and drew attention to the fact that birth and not death is seen as a tragic phenomenon . . .

If I am allowed to cite myself, I was questioned about JONAH in 1968.

'I was asked if the belly of the whale symbolized the journey in the cosmos or perhaps the interuterine loneliness. How far is Jonah the first or last man? Do you give a Freudian, mystical, political or cabalistic significance to this character? And in particular, what is the meaning of his final gesture? Isn't there too much bitterness? And aren't you sorry for humanity?'

Refusing to give the answers then, I won't, of course, do so now, out of a spirit of solidarity with the character, who prefers to define himself, allowing not even me into his territorial waters. Apart from literary and dramatic critics, the philosophers and sociologists showed most interest in the exegesis of these plays. Anything I could add now would only be a few details perhaps significant to fuller understanding. In the first staging of JONAH at the Small Theatre in Bucharest, under the then lesser-known theatre director Andrei Serban, something which I had not anticipated amazed me, yet which constantly recurred. As a young author, eager to be initiated into the phenomenon called 'contact with the audience', I went to each performance. One night, together with the director, I was watching through a kind of dirty window, or rather a crack in the wall at the back of the auditorium, the heroism of the tremendous actor George Constantin, who, in the whale's belly, was shouldering an immense role with brilliance and dramatic truth. The scenery was made from foam mattresses, difficult to climb, and the designer had dressed him in a white tunic made from goat skins. The massive, bearded actor sweated and lost pounds at each performance. What amazed me was that many people in the audience were crying. 'Look!' I said to Andrei, 'It's like a play for castaways! They're coming here to cry. Aristotle was certainly right about catharsis! But where have so many castaways come from? The battles of our troubled history have almost all been on land and we haven't lost many naval ones.' From this I concluded that the play addresses itself to mankind in general, and that it is contemporary although it gathers echoes, determinations, and hopes from the beginning of time, from the first venture into the open to fish, from the first slip of someone – prophet or ordinary mortal – down into the gullet of the whale.

'I am the whale,' I answered all those who had begun to ask me. (Just as Flaubert continued to be Emma.) 'And the first whale?' 'And the first whale!' 'Then who is the second whale?' 'Me again!' 'And the third?' 'Me again!'

The Hungarians produced a film of the play, the Danes, a film for television, following the play's successful performance with very interesting scenery: a theatre installed on an old ship in the middle of Copenhagen. The Finns, having a great fishing tradition, gave the part to a great actor who, with agile knife in hand, successfully conquered and let himself be swallowed by larger and still larger nets.

I've been told that a Polish theatre used the play, a short time after the premiere in Bucharest, as a means by which they could experiment in testing directors, actors and designers. Three different performances were given, each having a different director, actor and designer. The play was thus performed on three consecutive evenings and there were some avid theatregoers who insisted on seeing all three.

One more thing about JONAH. A translator from Buenos Aires, in all good faith, suggested an addition to the ending of a few lines written by himself in which Jonah indeed finds his way to the light and, transformed into a revolutionary, brings about social justice. I was told (this happened six or seven years ago) that this way it would go down better with the Argentinians and the Latin American public in general.

Beyond these happenings, which colour the biography of any writing, good or bad – writing which must however be kept in its true spirit, that of an artistic creation with a finality in its art, if it exists, the art being implicitly a reflection of reality, but no more than that – I would only like to add the author's dream (until now not realized anywhere in the world), that these three plays be performed one after the other in a single performance. They complement, answer and amplify each other, thus facilitating understanding.

After this trilogy I wrote other plays – a different style of theatre involving a different debate. I notice that so far in this preface, which threatens to turn into an evocation, my comments on THE MATRIX have been rather mean. (It's the only means an author has to escape from the undesirable explanation of his own work.) Not that I wouldn't have enough to say. A great deal can be said about a play with women it it! For example (to remain in the context of back stage detail), at the first staging in Bucharest, the director Dinu Cernescu, thought the part of Irina too difficult for a sole actress, although the role had been allocated to one of the most experienced actresses of tragedy, Leopoldina Bâlânutâ, so he divided the text into three – a sort of choir of young Irinas.

Indeed an interesting director's vision of the play, but quite distant from that of the author. In the play Irina is about to give birth at the same time as her father dies and the deluge begins. At this difficult moment, one had the feeling that instead of one birth there were three, yet only one death had taken place on stage.

The equilibrium I had thought out was no longer evident, and even more so at the end, when after three 'labours', the actress held only one child above the raging torrent.

However, this did not stop Cernescu's production of this play being one of the best and most successful of any yet staged in Romania.

I'm wondering if the main attraction for actresses is in fact the great difficulty and length of the part. The ones who have dared to act it have done so with great joy and excitement, and wouldn't have agreed for anything in the world to share the role with others. I saw the play at Geneva, at Dortmund (staged by the same Dinu Cernescu), at Helsinki, and at Katowice in Poland, and each time I was very impressed by the exceptional creativity of great actresses.

I drew my inspiration from real life – the catastrophic floods in Romania in 1970 – which set me an example of anonymous deeds of heroism and self-sacrifice. This event, the trigger of the play, pointed continuously to the symbolism of the flood.

With this play the author has already left the framework of monodrama; loneliness is conquered, even if in the final moment only one character is left alive.

Thus I finished a stage of creativity. I might write other monodramas, but into these three attempts I put many of my own thoughts. Out of that creative struggle, illustrated just as much in the poetry written during those years, a sizeable quantity of my soul's filings were thus attracted by the generous magnet of the theatre which opened before me like a bewitched horizon.

How shall I end?

My friends Andrea Deletant and Brenda Walker, working with so much passion to transpose the plays into language worthy of those famous English names to be found in the Encyclopaedia Britannica (to avoid mentioning one name as is customary and so doing an injustice to the others), have persuaded me to write these lines as a preface by showing me the cover devised by them for the proposed book: an icon on glass.

I don't usually write prefaces, I only just have time to create with terrible torment what normally follows a preface, but the thought of depositing my writing under such a fragile brow of a naive icon on glass, of the type painted centuries ago, and even today, by Romanian master-painters and carried in a bag to be sold at fairs, where they drink to seal the bargain, and peasants haggle for wool, goose feathers, corn and dried fruit – such an idea beckoned me.

I have allowed myself a slight alteration. The name of the author was placed on high, perched among the rays of resurrection between the sun and the moon – an unhappy position foreboding suffering. I have moved it to a more suitable and modest place (since one couldn't quite abandon the signature) down into the belly of the whale – earth.

My characters are irrevocably contemplative, forever unprotected in life, entirely unarmed from a pragmatic point of view – so I tell myself. They couldn't cross the Channel other than on a miraculous husk of a flask, more fragile that the egg of a swallow, forgotten under the eaves of a peasant's home. Not a sterile egg, but just delayed, the birth within it postponed, yet imminent. Whenever I look at the sky in autumn, when the migratory birds leave geometrically towards warmer climes, I seem to see in the flocks of storks, cranes, cuckoos, quails and blackbirds – an egg: towards the tail, flying as best it can, with inner wings, trying to keep up with the flock, asymmetrical and stubborn, sustained and pushed by who knows what mysterious forces, and by perhaps non-existent currents. And I'm thinking it will be born and come into being *in flight*. And it will return in spring to rest in its nest – the egg from outside the world and the awaited fledgling.

Marin Sorescu

Jonah: Finnish production, 1971.

JONAH

A tragedy in four scenes

CHARACTERS

JONAH, the fisherman

FISHERMAN 1
FISHERMAN 2   ageless extras

Like any very lonely man, Jonah talks aloud to himself. He asks question and gives answers, behaving all the time as if there were two characters on stage. He 'splits' and then 'contracts' himself back according to his inner life and stage demands. This 'pliable' part of the character should be acted with great flexibility and simplicity. If the role is too difficult, another actor may play the last two scenes.

Scene 1

The stage is divided into two. Half represents the enormous mouth of a fish and the other half the water, which is represented by chalk circles.

JONAH *sits carelessly in the fish's mouth with a net thrown over the circles. He has his back to the darkness of the mouth. Next to him there is a small aquarium containing a few tiny fish, which appear to move their tails cheerfully.*

JONAH: Now they're beginning to . . .
I think I can hear them . . . plop, plop, plish, plopping in the net.
Feels like boulders.
'Cos we've got a rich sea.
What a rich sea we've got.
I don't think they'll be long now.
Don't worry! [*He calls*] Jonah!
[*Hoarsely*] Jonah!
Nothing.
Wilderness.
Even a wilderness should answer me: an echo?
[*Realizing that there is no echo*] Hey, no echo?
[*Calls again to confirm his suspicion*] Jon . . . ah [*Waits*]
[*Wringing his hands in despair*] Even my echo's gone.
Vanished . . . finished.
That's gone as well.
A bad sign.
No, it could be a new move by the fishermen.
[*Illustrating his point*] This noise on the sea must stop at once.
What a racket!
It's not right to howl at sea.
On land it's passable.
But not at sea.
I cry out, you cry out, someone else cries. Noises gather.

3

The waves start to vibrate.

Like a bridge, where soldiers march all in step, it caves in.

Well, when that lot cross over!

And so with the sea. One wave starts vibrating, then another. A storm could start!

And when all that water caves in on us . . .

It's really not right for everyone at sea to cry out at the same time . . .

Even if they're shipwrecked?

Even the shipwrecked. They can all call, but in turn.

I see, so it's not noticed . . .

Otherwise one might think it was a full wake.

The sea would get angry.

[*Wisely*] That's why everyone must mind their own business.

[*Looking into the water*] Look in their own circle.

And keep quiet. [*Pause*]

But I have to shout. To call Jonah.

[*Calling*] Jonah!

Nothing.

[*Calling*] I don't want to catch you here. Do you hear me, Jonah? Stop following me about. [*He pauses*]

Actually I'm Jonah. Shhh! Don't let the fishes find out. That's why I call, to mislead them, because you see, Jonah's unlucky and that's all there is to it.

The fish have to think he's fishing somewhere else. Anywhere, God knows where!

[*Laughing*] I think he ought to fish in another sea. Maybe there . . .

But do you really think you can change your sea?

Ah, no way.

[*Shouting*] Jonah, keep away from this place or you'll frighten away my good luck!

[*Pulling out the empty net*] You already have.

[*Throwing the net back again*] What a rich sea we've got!

I've no idea how many fish are swarming around here.

[*Curiously*] How many do you think?

God knows – a lot.

[*With amazement*] A hundred?

More than that.

As many as you could count in a lifetime?

Even more.

4

Then as many as you could count in a deathtime?
Maybe, because death is a very long time.
What a long death we have! If you count such wealth in it, what a
rich sea we've got!
And how can the sea keep all these fish on food and drink?
It manages. With difficulty, but it manages.
[*Laughing*] I bet it's only water!
No, they don't drink water.
Well, it could be pouring them water as well.
When it sees them all with their mouths open . . .
[*Trying the net again*] It seems to be heavier now . . .
I think I've caught the big one.
I've been watching out for this fish for a very long time. I've even
dreamt about it.
That doesn't mean anything. I dream about fish every night.
Only of fish.
Maybe because my job's a . . . [*He gestures to indicate fishing*]
But I'm fed up with stench in my sleep.
One dream, one fish.
Dream one – a carp.
Dream two – a sturgeon.
Dream three – a herring.
At that herring, I always wake up cursing. I toss and turn in bed
until nearly morning, then I doze off again, and . . . what do you
think I dream about?
[*Curiously*] What?
Guess.
A whale?
No, I'm not that lucky. Go on, what do you think I dream about?
[*Even more curious*] What?
[*Sorrowfully*] Daphne.
Daphne?
Daphne, a crustacean so small that . . .
You can't even recall it.
It dissolves before you wake.
And it's the same every night, ever since I can remember.
And you still call that a dream?
No. I can't call it a dream anymore.
And all this time my two children sleep like logs.
How can some people sleep like that?
I asked them once: I said, "Here you two, what do you dream

5

about that you can sleep like logs?"
And they both answered, eyes sparkling with happiness: "The sea".
Pah!
It's all right for them, they dream about the sea *without* any fish.
Yet the sea is damned beautiful when you look at it.
That's what they dream, leaving me all the worry of the fish.
[*Sadly*] If I was a forester, after a time, there'd be only trees in my dreams.
I'd like to become a woodman and from my first night dream of a million trees.
And I'd rest in their shade.
In my sleep I'd sit in their shade.
What a thick shade a million trees would give.
Thick as honey.
And I, head on a root, looking for squirrels.
You mustn't catch squirrels.
That's *all* I'd need, to chase squirrels in my bloody sleep as well.
[*Looking in the net*] Is it . . . .?
Well, shall I pull it out?
[*Uncertain*] How can I be sure it's the right moment?
Why is the net so heavy?
The Devil himself . . .
I've been waiting for it for a long time . . . I even know what it looks like. It's got a mouth like that [*Involuntarily indicates the large fish mouth on the set*]
Ah, I've been waiting for it a long time.
I'd know every scale of it.
If it showed itself to me in the night!
For the last few years it's been in my head, it's just that I can't seem to land it here, in the net.
[*Giving himself courage*] Please God, help me! [*He pulls the net*]
Heavy, so heavy . . .
[*Pulling it out*] Nothing? [*He is amazed*]
Nothing.
Then why the hell did it weigh so much?
[*Looking at the horizon*] Ah, I see! That cloud. It's cast its shadow right across it.
I'd best start fishing for clouds.
One today, another tomorrow. I'd soon bring the flood.
Because I'm lucky with clouds. [*Pause*]

6

[*Catching sight of the aquarium, he talks to the small fish.*]
It's still in you that I put my hopes.
Poor little fishes.
They carry all the burdens of seas and oceans.
[*Pointing to the aquarium*] They're mine. Private property.
[*with sympathy*] They've already been caught.
I keep them on my windowsill as the light does them good. It contains all kinds of goodness. It fattens them, cheers them up.
[*Sadly*] It's just that it doesn't set them free.
[*Afraid*] How can it?
I'm a fisherman and I have to have fish in my house at all times. Or what would people say? When I feed them in the morning I stay just like this, watching them. Sometimes I stay for hours. My wife, who loves me, says "If you don't feel like going to catch more, stop looking at them like that, or *they* might die as well." I wouldn't be surprised if they did die because I watch them. I have a poisonous stare. Everything I set my eyes on dies. That's what she says.
Go on, I don't believe you, or she'd have been dead too, oho . . . long ago!
But they will all have to go in the end, because every time I go fishing, I take the aquarium with me. And when things have gone too far, and I've wasted a whole day in vain, I get the fishing rod out . . . [*He does so*] . . . and cast it into the aquarium [*Casts it in*]
When the first one rises, I'll throw the net in.
Because it takes so long to catch one [*Watching the float*] Now they're starting to go for it . . .
Mind you they take a long time to bite, because they've been caught before . . . but in the end one of them is bound to bite . . .
Not much water . . . the need for food continuously growing . . .
Can you ignore needs?
To be honest. I don't want one to bite just now.
That's impossible.
It's as if you'd drunk poison and thought it would have no effect. I'm sorry for them.
Fishes, take care, my bait will have an effect!
[*Watching the aquarium and then the sea*] This water is full of bait, all sorts of beautifully coloured bait. We, the fish, swim among them so fast, that we seem noisy. Our golden dream is to swallow one, of course the big one. We set our minds on

happiness, on hope, at any rate on something beautiful. But after a few moments we notice with amazement we've run out of water. [*With the solemnity of a choir*] Oh, fisherman who stands upon the shore, at least leave our way to it clear, don't darken it with the shadow of your legs.

[*Pauses, looking at the aquarium*] However, I can't help it. I've got to live as well. Come on you lot, have you started to bite yet? [*He leans over the aquarium and at that moment, the mouth of the huge fish begins to close. Jonah tries to fight off the jaws which are clenching and creaking with a terrible sound*]

Help! Heee . . . lp!

If only there was an echo!

DARKNESS

Scene 2

The interior of fish No 1. One can see fungi, little bones, algae, aquatic residues etc. The impression should be that you are at the bottom of the sea while at the same time there should be a suggestion of the interior of a huge belly. If possible, corners of the set would move rhythmically, opening and closing as if the fish digests.

The scene begins in semi-darkness. JONAH *stands centre stage, feeling about with his hands, dazed.*

JONAH: Am I mistaken, or is it late?

How time has flown!

It's beginning to get late in me. Look, it's grown dark in my right hand and in the acacia at the front of the house. I must put out with an eyelid all things which stayed alight, the slippers near the bed, the hallstand, the paintings. As for the rest of life's belongings, everything that can be seen, even beyond the stars, there's no point in taking those with me, they'll continue to burn. And in remembrance of me, I've left word that at least on more important feast days, the whole universe be given to the world – as alms. [*He pauses*]

8

However, I'm not too sleepy.

It doesn't matter, you have to sleep.

Why do people have to go to sleep at the end of their lives?

[*Urging himself*] Come on, put your head down. [*He attempts to do so, and at this moment the light comes on suddenly as if Jonah's idea*]

That's it!

The fish [*Realising the whole situation*] The fish, the fish . . . [*He is speechless. There is a short pause*]

I've been swallowed.

What, all of you?

[*Examining himself*] All of me.

Swallowed alive or . . . [*Hesitating*] . . . dead?

Well, since I'm aware . . .

[*Supporting his own belief*] I can walk, look, I can walk over here. [*He walks in one direction until he bumps into something and can go no further*]

[*Turning round calmly*] And I can walk there. [*He walks the other way and the same thing happens*]

I can walk wherever I like.

I do what I like. I can talk.

Let's see if I can keep quiet as well. If I can keep my mouth shut. [*He tries*]

No, I'm too afraid. [*He freezes centre stage. There is a pause.*]

Once I heard a story about someone who was swallowed by a whale.

[*Surprised*] Really, you don't say?

He was out fishing when this big whale came along and . . . gulp! [*He illustrates in sounds*].

What, finished?

It swallowed him.

[*Terrified*] And was he able to get out in one piece? How?

That's what I'm wondering. How does it go, and was there a moral?

I don't know, I only heard that bit, the first, which teaches us clearly that it is possible to be swallowed by a whale.

That's something I needn't have learned.

I could've found that out here! Why waste time on it? Why do people waste their time on things that are useless after death? I'd have been more interested in the rest of the story. [*Pauses*] He might have got away. Perhaps he stepped back, took a dive and

passed clean through the fish's belly, whistling. [*He whistles for a while*]
As for whistling, I can whistle too.
[*A little fish falls onto the stage*] What, has dinner come already? In some places you eat a lot in the morning and very little in the evening.
[*Another fish arrives*] It must be dinner time!
[*Another little fish arrives*] Oho! [*Taking the net and putting it in place where the fish are falling*]
Maybe I'm luckier now after such events.
[*Waiting a few moments*] No chance! More kicks than . . . .
[*Smiling*] I can see it starving as well because of me.
Better off left alone. [*Now about ten fish land in the net*]
[*Not able to deny the evidence*] However, progress is progress.
Ah no, no one is going to deny that.
[*Putting his hand to his head*] It's just that I don't feel so good. I can't enjoy it as I'd have liked to.
I'm not quite myself. [*He stumbles*] I wonder why?
Perhaps life, or the sun . . . because I waited a long time in the sun to land it. [*Indicates the big fish*]
I'm very curious to know if that man ever came out of the whale. I don't think so. Who'd ever come out at a time like this?
Is it raining? Water's always moving in nature, always moving. [*Looks towards the corners of the set which 'digest'*] And the fish, look at how it's all working. If that's the case, let me help you, so you don't grind on air. [*He takes a small fish from the net and holds it in place where the digestive movement is strongest. While the fish is stripped of flesh and consumed, he sings funerally . . .*]

> Eternally remembered,
> Eternally consumed, eternally consumed

[*He repeats it about six times*]
[*Jonah turns to the audience. There are tears in his eyes and then suddenly he bursts into laughter.*]
It forgot to take it away from me. [*He continues to laugh*]
[*Pulling out his knife*] That's what comes of swallowing me in such a hurry!
It should've had a sieve.
A grid or something.
There should be a grid at the entrance to every soul.
So no one can get inside it with a knife.

10

[*To the fish*] You silly fool. How could you overlook such a thing?

[*Handling the knife*] What if I were to kill myself?

[*Feeling for his belt*] Or would you prefer me to hang?

I've nothing to hang from. Your ribs keep moving. There's not a stable wave around here. The sea is caving in. They'd all fall on my head.

[*Pauses, then with a change of tone*] But the knife. He could've taken it away.

Or maybe I'm the first fisherman he's ever fished for. He could be young, inexperienced. You bump into young ones everywhere. That's normal isn't it?

Of course.

Otherwise there'd only be old folks.

[*Pondering upon this*] You know I don't think he's been through a lot of water.

[*Laughing*] I should have looked at his teeth.

In fact, we should consider everything. [*Looks for a place to stab the fish*]

I wonder where it's thinnest?

I was once on a mountain and the air there was so thick that I looked at it. You could see it. I stayed half an hour watching that air. The way I saw all the cells, it looked flawed.

You're not in the mountains here you know, you're at the seaside.

[*Continuing with his earlier thought*] You also felt like opening your pores. You even felt like opening your veins so you could feel it rushing in through every surface. [*He breathes in deeply*]

So . . . [*Then appears unwell*] It's so difficult to breathe . . .

And who would be so stupid as to open their pores now?

No one would be so stupid as to lay themselves open now!

Can't you smell how it stinks? It's bad enough breathing it in . . .

I've heard that some do quite the opposite and shutter their pores.

Good for them. Clever! [*He still feels unwell*] Oh, I don't know what's the matter with me. Open the window a little will you?

Which one?

Ah. They didn't make a window. I wonder where it'll be thinnest? I'll have to break the wall . . . [*He staggers across the stage*]

The only thing I'd make, if I had the means, would be a wooden bench in the middle of the sea. A grand construction of planed oak, so that the more cowardly seagulls could rest on it during a storm. It's exhausting keep pushing the waves from behind, giving them a kind of madness; better for the wind to settle there from time to time, and, thinking of me, say: "He never made anything worthwhile in his life apart from this wooden bench, putting the sea all round it." I've given it a lot of thought, and that is what I'd really like to do. Oh, what a sanctuary, to sit head in hands, in the middle of the soul.

DARKNESS

Scene 3

The interior of Fish No. 2. The set is similar to the previous one with the addition of a few items which would suggest evolution. On one side of the stage is a very important prop – a small windmill. (It does not have to be set in motion.) JONAH, *who is sucked towards it as if by a whirlwind, always guards against getting caught in the wooden sails.*

JONAH: It must have been waiting a long time.
   [*Reconstructing the scene*] I can almost see the deceased; it had just swallowed me and, with its belly full, was retreating some-place to consume me. To relish me.
   Satisfied, it was going along through the water, a little absent-minded, yet, careless as it was, it waggled its tail.
   It was definitely waggling its tail, because that's what they do when they're happy.
   But this other one, which had been watching it for a long time . . .
   Roughly how long?
   How should I know with fish? People can bear a grudge even for a lifetime. Well that's another story. We humans have our patience better trained, more highly developed.
   But he was a fish and starving.
   Perhaps it also wanted to waggle its tail.
   Let's say it'd been waiting for it for the last two days.

12

Maximum three.

So, as I said, while swimming, burping, suddenly . . . "Gulp"

[*The set appears to shake*] Oh! What's happening on the other side?

[*Unperturbed*] Ah! Events!

Perhaps by the time I leave things will become clearer.

[*Laughing*] By the time I get 'born' from here.

[*Afraid*] What if I'm dead and the question of my coming into the world arises again?

Nonsense!

Can't you see how everything gets confused?

It's the children talking in their mothers' wombs.

Do you mean to say that I too . . . [*He leaves it unfinished*]

Go on with you!

But I think I'd be able to : I know myself well enough.

There's a limit to everything.

[*Moving closer to the wall to measure himself*]

In any case, I'm too tall.

Unborn children can talk to each other as well.

Only twins. Pregnant women get together so the babies can chat a little. So they say.

To set the future right. [*Pauses. Jonah walks across the set and then stops horrified.*] What if I'm a twin?

Who with?

He's here. It's just that I can't see him.

[*Examining himself*] I should have got glasses long ago.

You neglect to do it day after day and never get to see your own brother.

The twin.

Two is a number . . .

FISHERMAN 1 *and* FISHERMAN 2 *enter. Each carries a plank of wood across his shoulders. They are silent.*

Four! Now we're four! [*As he approaches the fishermen he recognises them*]

You as well? If I hadn't recognised you, I'd have thought . . .

How are you?

FISHERMAN 1 *and* FISHERMAN 2 *withdraw to a corner of the stage and stand still and silent with the planks across their shoulders.*

13

Otherwise it wouldn't have been long before I'd have gone mad.
It's narrow in here, but it's still possible to lose your mind. It's not
very difficult.
In fact it's dead easy.
Because there are some conditions . . .
Some? All!
But look, because there are two of you, you've encouraged one
another. [*Imitating their conversation*]

    "Hey, don't give up, Son." "No, I won't, Mate"
    "Hey, don't give up, Mate." "No, I won't, Son"

[*He pauses*] And look where you've got to. You're damned lucky!
[*Curiously*] So, what was it like?
What a fool I am to ask. Many have gone their separate ways.
And will continue to do so.
That's what's been said.
But I'm going back home.
We'll go together. [*Laughing*] Or would you rather laze around
here a bit longer.
[*Laughing louder*] Are you onto a good thing here or something?
Answer me.
Why are you holding back?
Have you come to an arrangement as to the time you're to stay
swallowed?
Well how much longer?
An obligation? To whom? Who is responsible for your return?
For our going back?
We enter where we like and leave when we like.
And that's that!
Hmm! Now I come to think of it, no one's told me anything about
staying or leaving.
I'll leave this corpse of corpses.
[*Confidentially*] Because I've already left one.
And now, because I've started along this path . . .
Eh? What do you think?
I see, I see. What shall I tell them at home? When I get back to the
village they're bound to ask . . .
Leave it to me, I know what to say.
That you're well. Even this whale isn't as bad as people think . . .
And you're managing quite . . .
Well, well, even . . . fairly well. [*Nudging an imaginary woman*)

Be quiet woman. Why do you keep whining? Can't you hear, your husband's alive. What the hell? These eyes have seen him.
Alive like me, do you hear?
He couldn't come now, 'cos he sprained his ankle.
Dead tired.
And it's taken him too far out. As he was light – it kept on going with him it its belly.
And with his neighbour.
Both of them very thin.
That hawk carried them and even made the sea wonder: 'Hey, you! Where are you going? Where are you taking them?'
To the back of beyond.
Come on, stop crying. They've even built themselves a little house. You know, to recover a little.
[*Caressing her*] Come on, stop in now, 'cos in a day or two you'll find him here with you. He's bound to come. He might even be on his way now.
But as far as marriage is concerned, he said you can marry again. [*Pauses*] So at least you'll have some comfort.
"Let her get married," That's what he said. "'Cos I," he said, "I can't ask more of her." What a good man.
"When I get there, to that seashore, damn it, I'll do nothing but lie in the sun."
He wanted so much to lie on the sand again.
To dry out his bones
You see he had . . .
A wretched job . . .
And the whale hasn't helped. It's not too bad inside, but what dampness! . . .
What can you do?
Can you stop it?
The whale lives in water so the damp gets at it, seeps into it.
Hard luck if there are people there!
[*Irritated*] Then it shouldn't eat them, if it hasn't the right conditions!
You're talking nonsense.
It's got to live as well, hasn't it?
We've all got to live.
That's what I was saying – they all live . . . somewhere, wherever they are.
And you won't even know when one evening you'll find yourself

15

with them knock, knock, knocking on your window.
[*To the two fishermen, who are still standing silently on stage*]
Leave it to me. I'll sort it out, don't you worry!

The FISHERMEN *nod their heads as if reassured, and exit.*

Stupid me! I kept chattering on and they might have had work to
do!
Well, since they had those planks on their backs . . .
[*Angrily*] It's even making them slave away at it.
How hard it is to earn a bite to eat.
[*Pondering*] I too must get on with my own things.
[*Gets out the knife and begins to cut a window at the back of the
set*] If windows don't exist, we should invent them. [*Drops the
knife and is about to pick it up when he changes his mind*] How
about nails? Why do they grow like the nails of the living, and not
of the dead? [*He scratches with the nails of his right hand where
the knife had begun. There is a sound like a saw.*] They're like
knives! Well, with ten knives it's a different matter. [*He sets to
work with both hands in a casual manner as if he were using two
saws.*]
[*Smiling*] I could've broken this drum with just my eyelashes.
[*With realization*] And instead of eyelashes, I've got nails.
And instead of hair on my head, I have nails.
And instead of myself, I'm every inch a nail. A strong, untamed
one, like the one in God's foot. A nail which breaks the shoe leather
and appears to the world as a naked sword.

*The back panel of the set now collapses with a great noise. It becomes
dark for a few moments, to enable the panel to be removed revealing
the inteior of Fish No. 3 which lies behind the back set of Fish No. 2.
When the light reappears* JONAH *is disorientated for a few moments,
then he considers the situation, calmly.*

Another.
I might've known it couldn't end so soon.
Be still!
[*With feigned calmness*] Another one.
[*Calmer still*] And so still!
[*Erupting*] How long before a sea in turmoil? [*Pauses*] . . .
[*Bending down to watch something*] Beetles have a lot of legs, but

when they roll over they can't get up again. They're as good as dead. Maybe they ought to have some legs on their backs, to distribute them more rationally.

Ah, that's impossible. First they'd have to start a war for the redistribution of legs [*He stoops to pick something up, but is disappointed at what he finds.*] It's only a poor scale. I made a mistake.

[*Apologising*] Can't you see how dark it is?

[*With slight regret*] The other one seemed a bit brighter!

Don't speak so well of it here, in front of *this* one.

Now that it's swallowed it, I doubt if it matters anymore.

If it didn't matter, it wouldn't have swallowed it.

It could have made a mistake.

[*Not giving up*] It was more transparent. The sun shone through it a little from the water. It wasn't coated like this one seems to be, with old tiles covered in moss!

I wonder where that beetle's got to?

Actually it wasn't a beetle.

I don't know why I long to see a beetle.

Before, I used to like insects, all sorts of insects . . . I used to stay for thoughts on end watching them. That happened outside, when I was able to look at them.

There's a sort of insect like an ant. I don't know what they're called. [*Thinking*] No, I don't know what they're called.

They make small holes in the ground like a pin head. They move around and around the field for a while and then go back to their shelter.

How on this great earth can they each manage to find their own pin head of a hole.

Once, one of them was just getting ready to go down, when I took it away on my horse, because I was riding, and then let it go a long way off, miles away, just to see if it could find its own way back.

[*Curiously*] And did it?

I don't know. I didn't have time to find out. Other events intervened.

That story with . . .

No, the war. I went to war.

[*Angrily*] That's just what happens. We're hampered as we go about our work.

I wrote to my mother at home to go and check the place out.

TSM-C

17

And?
She couldn't find it. An earthquake had moved it somewhere
else.
Aha! [*Pauses*]
Before, I used to think all the time about my wife. Now as days
go by, my wife is clouding over in my mind and my mother is
brightening. Like a well with two buckets. One goes down and
the other comes up. Now only my mother rises.
The return!
How clearly I see her!
Maybe at this very minute she's thinking about her mother. If
her grandmother were alive she might be thinking of her mother
as well. There are coincidences like that. In the life of the world
I think there must be a moment when all people think about
their mother, even the dead. The daughter about the mother,
the mother of her mother, the grandmother of her
mother . . . until you arrive at the first mother, great and
good . . .
What stillness then must be in the world!
In that moment, if someone cried for help, he'd be heard by the
whole earth.
[*Looking about him*] If there was an empty bottle around here,
I'd write a note, put it inside and launch it onto the sea.
Mother – I'd write – a great misfortune has befallen me.
[*Entreating, yet exalted*] Give birth to me again!
My first life didn't quite work out. It could happen to anyone.
Who can live as they'd like to? But maybe the second time . . .
If not the second, perhaps the third, if not the third, then the
tenth.
Don't let such a little thing frighten you but keep on giving birth
to me.
[*Pauses*]
We always miss out on something in life and that's why we need
to be born again and again. The soldiers especially miss out on
Peace. They're so used to sleeping through the noise of drums
and voices that at the first silence they open their eyes, opening
them so wide that grass and birds enter as into craters of
extinguished volcanoes. Sleepwalkers miss the unseen moon,
waking in graves, treading gently on coffin lids, then climbing
onto the tip of a grass blade which hurls them towards the yoke
of that strange planet. [*He pauses*]

18

[*Looking round him again*] I could put my message in this bubble of bladder. [*He points towards a corner*]
[*Doubtfully*] Now . . . will it let me have it?
A bauble! It ought to be grateful I haven't started eating it from the inside [*He takes the bladder, looks at it, then with the knife cuts a piece of skin from his left palm, on which he then writes a few words with his own blood. The scene must be played as if it were a very natural thing to do. He then puts the 'note' into the bladder skin, inflates and ties it. Pauses*]
[*Explaining his behaviour*] It's man's duty to try.
I can just imagine them all leaping about with nets, fishing rods, harpoons, [*Imitating the bustle of a crowd*] piling into boats. The women with lanterns.
One day, two, as long as it takes.
Until groping, they find me.
If they had lanterns!
Still not possible, it's too thick.
True, the second one was thinner.
Shhh! [*He lies down on the floor of the belly*] Let's see you now, Laddie. You'll have to make sacrifices as well. Until they catch you . . . it won't be long now. I think they've been spotted already. How forgetful I am! I didn't launch my bubble. Now where should I . . . ? [*Knocks on the fish's ribs with his fist, to find out their thickness. He sighs*] Like the walls of Babylon. [*By mistake, he steps onto the bubble which bursts with an incredibly loud noise, like an explosion. Jonah, confused puts his hands to his eyes.*]
[*Uncovering them*] Where am I? We waste a quarter of our lives making links. All sorts of links between ideas . . . between butter- flies . . . between objects and dust. Everything flows so fast and yet we still link subject to predicate. We should take life and let it loose as it comes and stop trying to make links which won't hold. You know, while I'm babbling on, its as if I'm compensating for all those lost years of life.
[*He discovers the 'note' on the ground*]
I've even started to get letters.
Probably a castaway. They're apt to do this sort of thing.
Where there's sea – there are always shipwrecks.
[*Laughing*] He thinks I can save him!
Poor devils, they write and write.
The boredom!

[*Casting his eyes over the note*] He mourns like a child ... Let him stay in the other world if he whines like that! He had the misfortune to get into trouble and now he wants to move the heart of the world with his hapless fate ... so that everyone will drop what they're doing and start out on the waves! I tell you: not one will lift a finger. No one in the village. No one on earth, no one in heaven.

As large as this earth is, if this note was to pass from hand to hand, they'd all say you're right. But follow you into the sea? Not one of them!

Mankind couldn't give a damn about your fate.

[*Calmly*] What, when you were feeling fine, and you locked yourself in the house with your woman, didn't you ever shout from the rooftops you were happy?

And even if you had shouted, mankind couldn't have cared a damn about your happiness.

Manage the best you can, boy.

And at least don't trouble your mother with such bad news.

Let her think her son's all right, and that he's not afraid of loneliness. [*Throws the 'note' down, then pauses*]

I wonder why I got so angry?

I can't keep just to one emotion.

Like the moss on the tree, in one direction.

Sometimes I forget where I am and smile like this, without reason.

Sometimes I'm cheerful. [*He laughs*]

Very cheerful.

Because I forget about me. I lose myself somewhere, in some far distant place like forgetting a book on the window-sill.

Well, if only we knew where we stood all the time.

[*A tremor is felt on stage*]

The world is shaking like a rotten egg.

A rotten, putrid egg ...

From which some bright future should have emerged.

[*Laughing*] But it's changed its mind.

It must have been postponed.

The egg's gone off.

Now am I cheerful or ... ?

Half and half.

I feel a drowsiness coming over me ...

Like a gurgling jug filling up at a well. A dried up well. [*Pauses*]

What wilderness!

I wish God would come past here.

I'm longing to see someone walking down a road. To appear over there and to disappear here, taking just a few steps past me.

When I get out of here I'm going to stop the first man I meet and say to him, "How are you?"

I'm full of ideas.

Make sure you don't burst.

Like that bubble?

Worse – like all the bubbles all over the world.

Then at least it'll be a proper explosion.

Was the earthquake like the one that moved the bank where the insect pierced its nest?

It's so long ago, how did that spring to mind?

[*Looking attentively to one side*] Those eyes watching me, are they mine?

It's your imagination. There's no mirror around here.

[*Terrified*] They're real eyes. [*Starts to count*] One, two, three, a hundred pairs. And look, the other side as well, and there and there . . .

The stage gradually darkens obscuring movement in the corners.

Those are fishes behind the eyes.

Live fishes.

The offspring of the big monster. The unborn ones, carried in its womb. The explosion must have brought them to life and they grow now through fear. At night, in the forest, there is such darkness that trees grow through fear.

How large they've become!

They're moving towards me, mouths . . . [*Searches for the right word but can't find it*] with mouths . . . pulled from a scabbard . . . [*Shouting as in a nightmare*] They're eating me!

DARKNESS

Scene 4

The entrance to a cavity. The remains of the last fish split open by JONAH. *In front, rather like a beach, is some sand dirty with algae, and some shells. To the right there is a heap of boulders, some houses, and driftwood.*
At first the stage is empty and silent. Then at the entrance to the cavity, Jonah's beard appears, long, pointed and fluttering outside. It is like the beards of the hermits of frescoes. Jonah can't be seen yet.

JONAH: What a marvellous net I've got. I'd like to catch the sun in it now. Nothing else, just the Sun! [*He laughs*] And souse it to make it last longer.
[*He appears, hands to his eyes to protect himself from the light*] The sea. [*He removes his hands from his face*] The sea!
Air! [*Breathes in deeply to check*] Yes, this is air. [*Takes another deep breath*] Don't tell me there was air inside as well! No, don't tell me that or . . . I'll thump you.
Only I know what I've been breathing. Me and these nostrils of mine. [*Flicking the end of one nostril with his fingers*] Now they're beginning to awaken. [*Cheerfully*] Here out at sea, at the awakening of the nostrils.
[*Dilating his left nostril*] Come on, breathe now as you used to when you were young. [*He breathes in and out*]
And you, lazy one. [*He does the same with the other nostril*]
[*With emotion*] Real air.
[*Stretching out his right hand, fingers spread,*] I want to breathe a little with my palms as well.
It's all right, I know what I'm doing.
A little bit of ozone on my luck lines.
And a little bit of breeze. [*He pauses*]

The scene up to this point should be acted in exultation, almost like madness. Now Jonah begins to control himself.

How I waste time on trivialities.
[*Almost down to earth*] We must not waste time on trivialities.
Soon this corpse will sink . . . it will take on water.
[*Urging himself on*] To work!
What if I'm right in the middle of the sea?

22

I'll swim breaststroke one day, two, a year, until I'm tired, and then on my back, then on one side. Then in a finger, a strand of hair, a strand of soul, then in a breath, then in a sigh. I'll attain the end somehow.

[*About to throw himself in*] But where is . . . the sea?

There's not a drop of water to be seen.

[*Afraid*] Maybe it's evaporated. Maybe a flood of fire passed by and the sea stuck to its heels.

The sand shone and I thought horses were on the crest of the waves.

My eyesight's getting worse.

[*Gets down, and begins to walk*] A beach?

Maybe it's better this way. I doubt if I'd ever have succeeded on my own. [*Indicates the fish from which he has emerged*] And he did me a good turn.

Poor thing!

Don't keep saying "poor thing". I've told you once already.

I won't do it again.

It's good outside as well.

It's good everywhere.

All right, I know.

It's wonderful here.

I ought to be happy.

But I am.

No.

Really.

Perhaps later.

Yes, because happiness never comes when it should.

Who knows when I shall be glad of these important moments.

[*Smiling*] When I first kissed a girl – that was a long time ago – I felt nothing, apart from the taste of flesh. A taste of a cheek as if I'd kissed just another cheek.

I wasn't able to sense the difference, the thrill.

That's how it is.

Two days later, happiness came over me. Just like that, out of the blue.

In the end it dawned on me that it was through that kiss.

It's the same now.

I only feel I've stepped ashore and am going home.

I wonder where my house is.

I'll ask someone.

23

It's a bit deserted round here.
Where is everyone?
Fishing.
What else can one do? Stomach calls.
Both theirs and the fishes'.
Shut up!
I didn't mean to offend.
[*Calling*] Hey, good people! [*There is no answer*]
[*Calling again*] Hey, good people! [*No answer*]

FISHERMAN 1 *and* FISHERMAN 2 *enter with their planks still across their shoulders.*

[*Cheerfully*] You as well? That's good. How did you get out? I see you've brought your planks with you! Are your houses falling down, is that it? But, you mustn't injure yourselves carrying them from the world beyond. There must be some wood left around here as well, [*Laughing*] or do you want it [*Gestures to the fish*] to make a loss?

The set begins to shake and the two fishermen leave.

[*Suspiciously*] Why do I always meet the same people?
Has the world shrunk that much? The world's too small, at every step we meet only shadows – trees, birds, insects at every step. And with each one we have to be careful, saying hello to them, asking how they are and how they slept.
[*With sudden realization*] That's terrible!
I was wondering why I wasn't happy.
[*Climbs onto the pile of stones*] What can you see?
The horizon.
What is that horizon?
[*Horrified*] The belly of a fish.
And what lies beyond that horizon?
Another horizon.
What is that horizon?
The belly of a huge fish.
Look again. [*Jonah looks, then covers his eyes with his palms.*]
What did you see?
Nothing.
What did you see?
Nothing but an endless row of bellies. Like windows placed next to each other.

To be locked inside all those windows!

I'm like a God who can't be resurrected. All his wonders have succeeded, his coming to earth, his life, even his death – but once here, in the grave, he cannot rise again. He beats his head against the walls, calls upon all the powers of mind and wonder, driving himself into Godliness like a circus lion through a halo of fire. But he falls amid the flames. He's jumped through that hoop so many times that he never once imagined he'd stumble, particularly at the resurrection!

And everyone's expecting him above.

They all believe in him, some are even demented by so much faith. "Any minute now the tombstones will flower like the petals of a water lily, and the dead will rise, as is quite normal after so much waiting by mankind, and he will rise into Heaven to set us a shining example!" Because we, the people, ask for no more; just an example of resurrection. Then we'll go to our homes to die well, humanely, in our houses, in peace.

But first we want to see him.

While here he is, in the tomb, strength running out, with not enough voice to shout . . . "Good people, the resurrection's been postponed!" [*In a low impersonal voice*] On the seashore, a poor fisherman was fishing with his net for tiny fishes, and as he did so, the waters suddenly opened and a huge whale . . . [*He enacts the scene again. Pauses*] But who exactly was that man? And what was he thinking?

And why him?

Can you tell me that?

No one breathes a word . . .

That unfortunate one definitely hasn't succeeded in cutting open the huge belly . . .

[*Giving himself courage*] But I . . .

[*Thoughtfully*] The problem is, once born, is it possible to break out of anything. God, so many fish one inside the other!

When did they have the time to lay such a strata?

The world's existed for oh, such a long time!

[*Inspired*] Everything's a fish. We live inside the best we can.

Hmm! How naive I am. Perhaps I passed the place where I started, a long time ago. See, I should have marked it, then I would have stopped there and continued to live like everyone else. I wouldn't even have realized that everything else was floating. That's it! We should put a sign at each step, so we know where to stop just in case something happens. Not keep going on ahead. Not get lost ahead. [*Thoughtfully*] Outside . . . [*Changing his first thought*] However, such a place ought to exist. Maybe not large enough for all of you, but like I said, at least big enough to imprint your soles in it, for a moment. Then for someone else to come, with his soles burned by the night. And then another. Somewhere there should be such a place.

[*Ironically*] Prophet! A fine sort of prophet you've been! You envisaged your future very well. Now try and predict your past. Let's see if you can succeed in this at any rate, prophet! Come on, try and remember everything! [*He covers his face with his hands, stays like that for a few moments, then shakes his head. He cannot remember.*] It's so foggy!

Well, try to remember, at least something! [*He tries again*] What swirling fog!

[*Terrified*] I can't even remember a language in the wind. [*He pauses*] [*Shading his eyes*] What were those two good old people called, who kept coming to us when I was little? Or the other two, the sullen frowning man and the hardworking woman whom I used to see so often in our house, and who at the beginning weren't so very old? What was that building where I used to learn? What did I learn? What was the name of that square thing with four legs on which I ate and drank, and upon which I even danced a few times? Every day I used to see something round on the sky looking like a red wheel always rolling in the same direction. What was it called? What was that beautiful and wonderful, funny and wretched thing made from those years I've lived. What was my name?

[*Suddenly remembering*] Jonah.

[*Calling*] Jonahhhhhh!

I remembered: Jonah. I'm Jonah. [*Pauses*]

And now, come to think of it, I was right after all. I started off well, but the *road* was wrong. It should have gone the other way. [*Calling*] Jonahhh! Jonahhh! It's the opposite. Everything's the reverse, but I'm not giving up. I'll set off again and this time I'm taking you with me. What does it matter if one's lucky or unlucky. It's hard to be alone.

[*Getting out the knife*] Ready Jonah? [*He cuts open his own stomach*] Somehow we'll find our way to the light.

CURTAIN

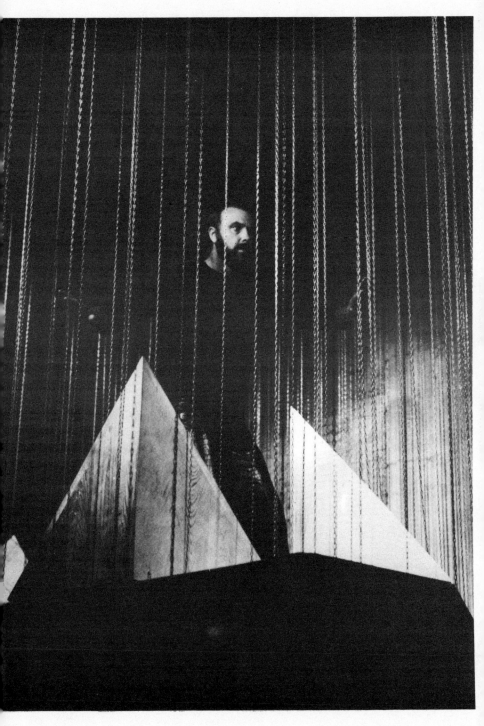

Jonah: Swiss production, 1970.

THE VERGER

A tragedy in three scenes

CHARACTERS

THE VERGER, a lighter of candles. He is younger at the beginning, older towards the end – how time passes!

THE WATCHMAN, deaf

The scenery is inspired by life in a cathedral. The last cathedral seen by the designer. Seen from the inside, with an attentive eye for the flight of Gothic style. A feeling of too much space, too little time.

On the rose window: 'The Four Seasons' by Brueghel the Elder, which will be seen from time to time with the help of a spotlight.

Scene 1

THE VERGER, *somewhere near the door, stares at it. It is as if he expects someone to enter. However, it is clear that no one else is coming to the cathedral. The man shakes his head, looks at the walls, shakes his head again, then walks towards the altar, returning with a candle. He puts it down, brings another, then another, and then a few armfuls.*

VERGER *[in the middle of the cathedral, with a lighted candle in his hand]*: It's as if a bee were burning . . . The flame soars heavenwards, the smoke sideways. It settles on the walls: a sign the flame has found its rightful path. Heavenwards. *[Looking around]* These stones are so – new. So unsmoked: they leer like devils' teeth.
[Sadly] Here no light has reached heaven.
[Slowly, with pain and slight guilt in his voice] My work is to light candles and . . . nothing more. I look after the candlesticks and the incense burner. I put a torch in people's hands, and no more. I retreat to a corner and watch them at prayer. *[Attempts to see them praying]*
[Scolding himself] Who do you expect to be praying?
[Moving the candle to the other hand, as if it had hurt him] No one comes here anymore.
[Laughing] Only I rushed in.
[Seriously] In fact I just found myself here. I found myself, candle in hand, singing 'Forever Remembered'.
[Searching in his memory] Ever since I've known myself, I can't remember seeing anyone else enter here.
[Secretly] It's a forgotten cathedral. People tired of building it, so that no sooner had they put the crest on the arrow of the weather vane, than they forgot all about it. They began forgetting it long ago, centuries ago, and at that moment the forgetting was sudden, total. *[Imitating them]* "Thank goodness that's finished" – they said, and started thinking about something else. At any rate, not about another cathedral. They no longer build cathedrals. This is the last. And I'm the last.

31

[*Laughing*] This Verger is the last one left . . .

[*Looks for a long time at the white walls*] My smoke isn't even felt . . . I wonder what they're saying, these stones: "The Verger's smoke – is nothing" . . .

[*Showing the candle's flame*] Now it's like water!

[*With a sign of disgust*] Now, if someone had anointed me verger, maybe . . . But no one told me to be verger, I just found myself here, suddenly, like that, for no reason. Thus self-anointments happen . . .

[*Apologising*] You know, this cathedral is forgotten, yes, very much forgotten, and I am a verger . . . of my own free will.

[*He takes a few steps*] I'm even frightened to walk at night on the stone slabs . . . Steps [*He listens*] echo . . . like a wilderness. A wilderness seems larger when you are walking through it. [*Meditating*] In a day or two this will also collapse. A new earthquake perhaps, or something, and then . . . It hasn't even had as many followers as a tortoise! He lives but a few centuries and yet has more of a smoke crust when he dies. Who the devil follows him around with a candle?

[*Looking for something at the foot of the wall, on the right, near the entrance*] There it is.

[*Stops in front of a darker stone*] Stone, tiny stone, I'll start with you. [*Laughing a little excitedly*]

[*He presses the candle to the stone and begins covering it with smoke*] The smoke nestles in the cracks. The stone grows moss and lichen, moss without lichen. The stone grows smoke.

[*Listening*] How time passes. Sfir, sfirr! [*He makes the noise of a burning candle*]

[*Pointing towards the smoked stone block*] I've settled on one more stone.

[*Exalted*] The flame has passed into glory, just like this one, and settled on a wall of fire – I work here in its shadow.

[*A new candle. Smiling*] We deceive the best we can.

[*Faintly, looking upwards*] Forgive me, for beginning to doubt at the very first stone.

[*Continues to work with some urgency*] It's better if everything happens in silence. The candle simply burns, I don't have to talk to it. The same with our breath, it's simply breath, a breath without comment. [*Pause*]

I thought I'd manage to complete this rock in less than a year.

[*Enviously*] All the soot in all that Gothic massiveness full of pipes! Well, they're so old, many centuries old. And they have so many generations on the walls . . . But me, I'm only one generation . . . [*As if to spite himself*] Like it or not, I don't know what's going on in other places . . .

[*Passes onto the neighbouring stone block*] I've laid the corner stone.

[*Laughs*] From now on everything will be much simpler. [*The next one*] If one day it could be established that, look, this is the centre of heaven, they'd all rush in here, pushing and even starting wars, outdoing each other, to settle here on the wall, to build houses . . . If you were to say – "This stone is the eye of God" – they'd all stretch out on the wall like lizards. "We're getting into your eyes, God, see us." But as it is, no one, and nothing to worry about.

[*Starting out of his reverie*] I'll get some more candles.

[*Walks towards the pile and looks around enquiringly*] I wonder how it gets in here? Where it's slipping away? Or maybe it drips, moment by moment like the tap of an unknown finger on the lump in your throat, swollen with fear.

[*Searching similarly upwards*] And from above, at the same time . . . I feel a whirlwind around my knees, guiding me to fall on them . . .

[*Meditating*] With their last breath, the dying could turn wheels of such strength that they would take our earth out of this ill-fated zone. Except that it hasn't occurred to them to blow at the same time. We die disorganised, and that's it.

[*Blowing*] Push this cathedral into another zone, a new one . . .

[*Blows again a few more times*] Can you? You can't!

[*Studying the walls*] The stones haven't yet been welded with the smoke of prayers. The rifts are alive.

[*Smiling*] And mystery creeps in where it can.

[*Pauses*] In the mouths of the dead there is a funnel where mystery is poured into the universe . . . But me, I'm only one generation . . .

[*Concluding*] It's wiser for us to be wary of our rock . . .

[*Returns near the stone block with a gesture of forgetfulness*] I was going for some candles.

Goes to the pile, takes two candles and creates a kind of lever. He puts a few candles on the end of it and catapults them upwards.

And now if I stretch this arm even more . . .

[*Staring somewhere*] Who are you, you at the end of the big lever, with a ray beneath your foot, which you hardly press with the pulse in your foot of air for the sun to spring to a rhythmic rising, because the arm of the lever is as long as eternity. You lean on it gently with your elbow, deep in your own thoughts and the earth rises to the leaf tops, to my top. The mountains start to turn in the vulture's crop; helping it to digest – because the arm of the lever is beyond imagination. And if we lengthen it more, there doesn't have to be anyone at the other end: the movement will continue of its own accord. A gentle breeze, a snap – the mechanism works alone. [*With the lever he projects them upwards*]

[*Solemnly*] I am watching – and stars rise on another planet. I speak and it thunders and lightens on another planet. I am weak as an ant, but on another planet my power grows fearfully. And I am a God there without knowing it.

[*Trying to minimize*] Look what's running through my mind! Eh, thoughts driven till the bitter shroud.

[*Stopping from his work*] I'd like to raise an anthem to that white linen. To that extraordinary white linen – until which we were meant to go on thinking. It can be made of clouds, of thin air, total abyss. We have to push ourselves that far. Hurling ourselves, destiny first. As far as the white linen . . .

[*Resigned*] After which we fall, broken and defeated to the bottom of our ship, to slave in the galleys. On the bottom of the coffin, to slave in the galleys.

[*Takes two candles, lights one*] Who'll help me slave in the galleys through this ocean of smoke?

Takes a few more candles, returns to work. For a while there is silence.

[*Technically*] The stupid ones absorb darkness greedily. Like dead eyes pricked by ants.

[*Attentively*] This one has just about had its share. Good. But I forgot the rift between them.

[*Welding it with a candle*] The right lines eat up so much smoke.

[*Getting an idea*] Shall I leave you like that?

[*With conviction*] I can't. If you leave rifts unsmoked, all the joint will collapse.

[*He sees a niche close by*] A niche! That's all I needed: It's like

pouring into the mouth of hell.
[*Works like a bricklayer, pushing in the smoke with his hand, and levelling it with his palm. He straightens his back and sighs*] Will I ever reach the altar?
[*Explaining as if to himself*] That's where the saints are . . .
[*Nostalgically*] All my life I've dreamt of lighting a halo.
[*Prays*] Saints, let me join your ranks, at least as an extra. You're getting old, perhaps you feel the pain of age painted on your bodies in so many stages. Let me carry out the humblest jobs in nooks and crannies. I could for instance eat the light at the Last Supper, and blow out your haloes when the service is over. And, from time to time, at half a wall's distance, cup my hands to my mouth and holler, once for the believers and once for the un-believers: Hallelujah! Hallelujah!
[*Loudly*] Hallelujah! Hallelujah!

Scene 2

The same set. The walls up to the height of the Verger, blossoming with burning candles. THE VERGER, *a stage older, walks backwards and forwards, here and there, straightening a torch or lighting a new one. Somewhere, in a corner, a bat hangs head down, with out-stretched wings, fantastically enlarged by the play of lights.*

VERGER [*Looking with admiration*]: Now, that's more like a cathedral. It needed a choir. [*Gesturing towards the candles*]
[*With emotion*] Now it's a cathedral in the true sense of holiness.
[*Listening*] It's as if the grass from outside is rushing in through the wall, grows through the wall. Like the arrows through Saint Sebastian.
[*Looking for him*] He must be here somewhere. He's listening as well to the grass growing through his wounds. To how he fills up with greenery.
[*Sadly*] We get old. Our age runs out. And we must fill up with something . . .

35

[*Smiling, as he walks past, through the torches*] I grow young again in the space between the candles. I grow old when I pass through fire, and regenerate again in darkness ... The same with him: he grows young in the space between the arrows, where he must feel omnipotent and strong. [*Pauses*]
And the world grows young in the space between the lights.
[*Indicating the flames*] Only the imploring hands of the crowd are missing, grasping them as they would stars, when the earth falls into darkness. . . .
[*Laughing slightly, looking at the walls*] I had to perform a small miracle. Miracles are accepted above if they are placed in the service of a great cause.
[*Solemnly*] Any minute you expect to hear a child's cry.
[*Waits for a moment*] However, I . . . if I tried to cry . . .
[*Attempts to do so*] I can't, my larynx is ossified, whimpers articulate themselves, become sinful words. Yet, wait . . . [*He lies down with the candle in his hand*]

Three butterflies, beautifully coloured, appear from the darkness and begin to rotate round the candle's flame.

Here come the Three Wise Men.
[*Following the flight of the butterflies*] Am I mistaken, or are they praying?

An organ sounds, singing of a choir is heard.

God, a light bulb is no longer enough for us. Everywhere we've licked it with our wings, on thighs, and on the mouth, and anyway we are the three of threes, if you still recall those travellers.
FIRST VOICE: "I, for one, have ploughed the field and for a long time have sensed this light. I even dreamed about it, nostalgically, on a sunflower."
SECOND VOICE: "I, the one on the right, come from I know not where, from the right."
THIRD VOICE: "I, the one on the left, come from I know not where, from the left."
CHOIR: "Now we circle wildly round the bulb, through all rays we are rulers over the laws of rotation, where we first set alight the pollen from the right, from the left, and from the centre of the light. Then we set alight our wings, whiskers of the Wise Men, leaving only

stumps of Magi. Small as butterflies. Worn out coming here, having blown warm in all the mangers, but found them . . . deserted. And now, look, just an old man in the last stable. [*Menacingly*] God, make sure we don't run out of hope before we run out of wings!"

The choir stops, the organ is silent. The Verger leaps to his feet, to find himself screaming.

Because nowhere are we given to understand that this pure and simple burning might be a miracle! [*With a nervous fluttering of hands, he puts out the candles*]
[*From the darkness*] God, perhaps a larger bulb, or something . . .

The next scene takes place in darkness. The bat detaches itself from the wall, and begins to fly about him. The man defends himself with his hands, calmly at first, and then becoming more and more afraid.

The fruit bat has blossomed. That's how trees ought to be in hell: with claws and wings. And when they bloom, hit you from all sides. [*He defends himself*] When history breaks off, prehistoric monsters appear.
[*Laughing loudly, in a sinister manner*] Jacob's fight with the angel!
[*In a normal tone*] Leave me alone, can't you see I'm not Jacob? I'm no Jacob!
Ah, I've caught you! You wanted to get into my hair, you devil! [*Afraid*] Ouch! It caught me with its horns. It's got horns too. I've lost it! Or is it me who has horns, is it me with claws, is it me who has black wings? Go away, bat, can't you see one is mistaken for the other? Or do I have to run, to fly, crucify myself head down on the first beam? [*Begins to shout*] The bat – it's entered my chest. I am an old belfry . . .
[*Solemnly*] . . . in the night, when I shake out the bats from me, like the forbidden tree of heaven, with devils right there on the branches. Leave them in the world, I say, to enjoy darkness as we do the light, a perfect equilibrium. For if we don't encourage darkness it will gradually weaken.
Leave them in the world, I say, to catch the insects on the wall, standing guard over the people. What other evil could they do? To make contact with the trees when they mistrust each

other . . . [*Pause*]
It's gone.
[*Waiting for it*] I come resonating with the dark and shiver in the darkness. I am made from emptiness which vibrates with the world, creating strange echoes, every time the world creaks without good reason. Or from a series of forgotten, forgiven, deadly sins, which vibrate at the rising of the moon. The tick-tock of things frightens me so much, that in vain I move further and further away. I start, as though awakened outside myself. I've heard that my heart will beat faster tomorrow, that's why I stay awake now pretending to talk or to be quiet, pretending to expect someone and that the noise doesn't frighten me at all.

Strange noises, fluttering of wings. He lights a candle, then in turn, all the candles on one wall. On the opposite side, the bat is seen in its original position, like a fresco.

[*Making shadows*] Just look at this!
[*With a strange voice*] The wall's gone mad! What's the matter with it? I can see three of my shadows there at three different ages. Never before have I cast three shadows on earth, the most was two, once on a Sunday, dressed up in new dreams.
[*Amazed*] There's another! It climbed right up. I'm the deepest sleepwalker above normal shadows.
[*With a crescendo*] What sort of holy light could collapse like this? It's true that all kinds of people died within walls. For so many centuries they were walled up and died. Maybe souls still exist which oblivion hasn't chewed enough, well remembered, maybe a fragment of an eye, or an eyelash, an ankle, now catches my ray, and takes my shape, content with my shape, just to be embodied once again.
[*Counts*] Three, four, five . . .
[*Gladly*] I've got as far as seven.
[*Scolding himself*] Why are you casting seven shadows on earth for nothing?
[*Sadly*] Now even if I walked on my hands, or my head, I couldn't go above seven. Everything has a logic . . .
[*Lucidly*] Everything has a limit and I can't fill the cathedral.
[*Continuing to smoke the wall for a while, stone by stone*] If only the organ could be heard! Something about ageing . . .

The altar begins to glow in the darkness.

It's beginning to shine. We've reached the altar, now we must
smoke the altar.
[*In exultation*] The darkening of the altar! I've reached here, tooth
and nail. Struggling with . . .
[*Sighing with relief*] A little breath blew over these walls. A little
mist . . .
[*Leaning with his forehead on the altar screen, tired*] Someone
once painted a church on a grouse. It was the last one in these
parts. All the rest had been hunted. As for the church – there
hadn't been one for a long time. So he painted one on the grouse.
Christ's wonders – on the crest, on the long feathery whiskers and
crop. The wings: on one the passion and the laying in the tomb,
the ascent to heaven on the other. This evens them out, so they
say. What you place in the grave with the left wing, you raise up to
heaven when you flutter with the right. And the reverse. What you
raise you place in the grave. A water mill with pails. He made the
grouse a church and set it free in the field. All day long he chased it
so that he might pray.
"Have you by any chance seen my church?" he asked everyone.
One day, he spotted someone going past with it hung from his
waist, bleeding . . . But I have my cathedral . . . Who could shoot
that. And how could that possibly be hung round a waist? Because
then I'd poke my head out of a window and roar to be
remembered, "Murderers!" [*He pauses*]
Let's see what else is written on the icons? You can feel the egg
yolk. [*Thoughtfully*] The saints emerge from the yolk, like para-
chutists from an aeroplane. As long as there's an egg, the wonder
will glide over us.
[*Attempts to see the painting*] There, my sight's failing.
[*He shades his eyes with his hand*] You pray for such a long time
for God to show himself, and then when you do get near, you can
no longer see Him.
[*Sighing*] Look, nothing is caught by my eyelids, when I press
them together. Only the air, lets itself be caught, like a sheep. And
I take pity on it, for how gentle it is, and the eye – leafless over it.
[*Prayer*] Thorn on the hedgehog of a burr, I crave with thirst for
holy wool.
[*Building to a crescendo*] Oh, that burr which lost its sheep on the
spur of Paradise, who comforts and who calms it?

39

[*Softly*] God, you are my lost sheep, without you, alone, I fear. Take me with you through your infinite world, or at least to the moon of your ear . . . [*Pauses*]
The prayers are heard more easily at the altar. Holy ears are here, and that means one cries straight into them. Just look now at this icon.

He lights another candle, to peer at the icon.

[*Surprised*] It's empty. There's only the frame.
[*Reasoning*] The painter hasn't got round to doing it. Something must have happened in the meantime. There is always room for something in the meantime.
[*Illuminating more frames*] In the meantime the painter became blind. Or, perhaps there was nothing to go in the frames – so he left them empty? Isn't there even a halo?
Look, if I clasp my soul, nothing gets caught in it . . .
Anyway, I've gone far, very far, as far as I could go . . .
[*Thinking with apprehension*] Can there be anything more?
[*Almost crying*] Trees grow, come into bud, loose their leaves and wonder: Can there be anything more?
People love, talk to each other and die. Can there be anything more? The dead remain silent. They scan eternity and remain silent. They let the grass make them optimistic till autumn. Then die again, over their old death, in a heap.
And they remain silent, silent, silent.
[*Showing with the candle the distance he has travelled*] At any rate, I reached the altar . . .
[*A moment of indecision, then calmly he continues to throw light onto the empty frames*] We should never be discouraged by so little. A candle must still be held, just as if nothing had happened.

CURTAIN

Scene 3

Along the wall scaffolding has appeared. At the beginning of the scene,
THE VERGER *might still be pottering about on it, to see if all is secure.*
The walls have been blackened as far as the dome where only a narrow
white strip remains. The man climbs there with difficulty, and
exhausted, starts to work again.

VERGER: It's beginning to smell of holy oil. Above the sinful earth a
layer of oil rises to the surface as oil will.
[*Stopping from his work*] I wonder if I could sleep on oil? To rise
above it all . . . [*Sighing*] . . . and roast forever!
[*Leaning with his forehead on the wall*] This burning light . . . If
anyone around here's awake, I'll go and ask him to close his eyes.
If there's a guard about, I'll force him to make peace. If under the
window a flower blooms, I'll watch it until morning.
[*Walking on the scaffolding*] I can't do anything to the stars. I've
calculated that I could sleep normally over a million eternities, till
a universal eclipse takes place.
[*Nervously*] But awake there's nothing I can do until then. [*He
continues to work*]
[*Almost happily*] There also exists a voluptuousness of exhaustion.
How strange must the well squeezed lemon feel! "Look, I'm
completely drained." [*He sighs*]

By chance he lights the painting of Saint Sebastian.

[*With surprise*] At last, a happy man!
[*Noticing the body torn by arrows*] . . . Who has taken his
destiny in his own hands, in his own body, in his eyes, his
heart . . .
[*Lighting up the ones who shot the arrows*] Although the distance
from which they shoot is rather small. You're not allowed to aim
at a saint from a distance less than three metres. It's not human!
Man is happy suffering, but one shouldn't overstep the limit.
[*Shouting to the pagans*] It's not human, you heathens!
[*To the Saint*] The next thing for me to do would be to drive the
villains beyond the dome, to untie you from this wretched tree, to
anoint your wounds and wash your feet! That would be justice.
It's just that nothing's in my power.
[*Sadly*] Although I'm alive and they are dead. Do you know what

41

I can do as a living man? Stay here and weep. [*He cries at the Saint's feet*]

[*Remembering something*] And, as far as I can see, it isn't even hell . . . Suffering outside hell . . . I don't know if it's accepted there.

[*Curiously.*] Can one suffer outside of hell? Is it allowed? Has it been generalized now? Anyway, I'll untie you in the end. Others in their turn . . .

[*Whispering in his ear*] . . . Saints are protected. When they're moved elsewhere, they are taken plaster and all. It's more difficult for people . . . Without the plaster . . .

[*Smiling*] I've set off alone with my plaster, to heaven. I'm looking for the wall. The wall, do you hear me?

[*Pointing towards the sky*] He's there.

[*As if to himself*] God made me a sign from heaven, a discreet sign, so that the rest of the world wouldn't notice. Me, being naive, was as usual, expecting lightning, and preparing to go to ground, because every time lightning strikes, I go to earth, charcoal, waiting for the electricity to pass away.

[*Raising his finger to his lips*] This time – He himself . . .

[*Frightened*] I don't know what will follow so I go on thinking, talking to the Saints, I shake my head normally . . . but . . . He gave me a sign.

[*Solemnly*] The gesture has been consumed and I don't know what to expect.

[*He passes on*]

[*Prosaically*] Oh, look at this, a really white stone. [*A sound of exasperation. Smokes it*] I dip the globe in smoke. [*He laughs*]

[*Angry at his own energy*] Words on walls.

['*Noting it*' *in his thoughts*] This as well . . . I should tell Him.

[*Coughs, which puts out the candle*] The smoke . . .

[*Lighting another one*] The wax – almost gone as well.

[*Furiously*] I've been calling that Watchman for ages to bring me some more! I still need a cartful or two if I'm to do a proper job . . .

I'll try again.

[*Calls*] Hey, Watchman! Watchman!

[*Resigned*] All in vain!

[*Confessing*] You see, he's deaf. He never heard me, and I . . .

[*Coughs again*] I didn't believe such deaf people existed in this world.

42

[*Wisely*] I was just talking to the first one painted in the nave. He kept me near him for a week. He liked the smell of the wax, it tickled his nostrils. "Good smoke," he said, "Where did you find it? It does me good, although I'm not allowed to inhale it!" "Maybe you can do something for the deaf as well," I told him. "No," he said, "all we can do is make them watchmen". [*Pause*] [*Remembering*] I was coming from behind, from nowhere . . . He was coming from nowhere as well . . . except that God had breathed upon him . . . which could be seen. The disaster had to happen anyway: The heavens had reached such a level of holiness, that anything you did, taking a bite out of something or not taking a bite out of anything, lifting a finger or not lifting a finger, was a capital sin.

[*Loudly*] The creation of the first men was the sign of total and absolute decadence in heaven.

[*Thoughtfully*] Victim of our desire to be born – blind, deaf, crippled, in whatever way, just to be born sometime, over a thousand, two thousand years, any time, no matter how.

[*Guiltily*] We used to be there somewhere, catching up behind. Out of nowhere. It was we who pushed Him from behind, opened His mouth full of shiny teeth and taught Him this child of the earth: "Bite and release the celestial atomism".

[*After a short pause*] And because of this, look what a watchman I've got!

[*Calling*] You, deaf one!

[*Resigned*] I'll have to manage on my own.

[*With an idea*] I'll hold the candle alight but it only needs to burn half the time. Then I'll put it out. The rest of the time I'll hold it extinguished.

[*Smiling*] To burn extinguished, to smoke the Saints by heart. About the flame hovers the possibility of being extinguished.

[*Blowing out the candle*] Gooood! Now we'll light it again!

[*Lights it*] We economise the best we can.

[*Explaining himself*] Because I can't come before Him without a whole candle in my hand.

[*Imagining*] He stays on the clouds, they're good quality ones, which hold him. They're clouds which don't rain when He wants a drought, such as a dry flood.

[*In a different tone*] The squirrels, jumping from one drop to the other, climb through rain to the dark cloud's crown. That's how I'd like to climb to the top, on my thoughts, where peace is

possible, because life and death would happen beneath me, like rain under the cloud. [*Pauses*] But as it is, I have to go from stone to stone.
All my life I've been looking for Him. Where are you, Tom Noddy?
Because you tied my eyes and I can only call you like this, like a child. [*Crying*] Where are you Tom Noddy? Even my bees are almost finished . . .
[*With vision*] This church drips with bees, which live only as long as the burning of a candle. Oh, they're happy in this little life, and continue to make honey, and a candle for bees of the future. The Saints try to throw off the germs brought here by the dead . . . Germs brought by the dead, germs which take refuge on the Saints, infuriated as well by past evils. There is a flurry on the walls, a shaking off of cloaks, while the people cry out and the dead are questioned. [*Loudly and with a deep voice full of echoes*]

> Why were you born?
> Why did you live?
> Why did you die?

[*Simply*] As easy as one, two, three, answer, dead one, faster, look at the chronometer in the hand of the referee, there in the belfry, who has stopped the game and holds your breath in his hand like a deflated ball . . . Look, the chronometer has already started to tick. You have just one minute for each question.

A *chronometer is heard.*

And the dead one keeps quiet and has retreated to the corner of the left eye, forgotten there since the day before yesterday.
[*Coldly*] So, the dead keep quiet and the chronometer suddenly tolls, shown to be a bell, and the tear of the dead man bursts. And the germs invade the Saints even more, who try to adapt to the situation. And the plaster begins to crumble . . .

At *the last words, the chronometer changes into the toll of a bell.*

[*After a short pause*] And I, what must I do about all this? My death's my own concern.
[*In the tone of a prayer*] What must we do, we the others? The many, yet the others! After you've done everything alone, what is

there for us, the ones on the bottom of completed things? If we could at least rain back the flood, throw it back upwards, in forty days and a million nights, punishing you for your sins! Or to snow it, and fly, each riding on a snowflake towards stars greedy for snow! And in hibernation to snow you up, as before creation, and to spring through your mind like avalanches through a dream. And for you to think us up, each one of us from the beginning. And to change your mind about us from the beginning. And not even to create us again. And to leave us alone! God! [*Shouting*] Leave us alone! Bloody hell, leave us alone!

The door of the cathedral opens with a prolonged creaking. The Watchman enters.

WATCHMAN [*cleaning out his ear with the key. He spots the scaffolding*]: Here!
[*Goes out and returns with some tools. He begins to dismantle it*]
VERGER: [*on high at his work*]: I can almost touch Him. But how this candle flickers! Oh, if I had a little more wax! [*Calling to the Watchman, whom he can't see*] Hey! Hey you!

The Watchman doesn't hear. Pulls a plank or metal bar, or something and the scaffolding collapses from the top. He exits.

VERGER [*floating in the dome above with his candle, like a miracle*]: Now I hold it longer unlit, I blow on it, my breath warms it and gives out a sort of mist, which settles on the walls. If only I had the strength to finish this foundation!
[*Encouraging himself*] It's not long now, I'm close to the arrow rising like a finger with something to say.
[*Curiously*] I wonder what it would say?
[*Drained of strength*] If your eyelids don't hurt you when you close them. If your eyelashes don't rattle, like two curtains of poisoned spears. If the darkness doesn't stifle you every evening, like a door which catches your hand, then ankle, then neck. If the teeth don't poison you when you swallow them every time you inhale, putting them back when you sigh, in an eternal boxing with infinity . . .
[*Suddenly deciding*] I'm doing nothing else to finish it. Let me get down, I can't make a church any blacker than this one. So don't be afraid . . .

[*Motions to descend*] Slowly, slowly. Let me hold tight to the scaffolding. [*Notices that it has been taken away*] The steps! Quickly, the steps! I'm falling ... I'm returning down to the foundations, deep, near the Holy Fathers.

I'll lie down next to them, pull up a slab to cover my head, an old slab, with the writing a little faded, so that nothing more can be read, but a succession of letters, which, no matter how hard they try, can't be made into words again. And it will be fine like that ... Because it will be quiet – and nothing will be noticed.

[*Notices that he is floating*] Then I'm not falling.

[*Annoyed*] It's not possible ... My body has the right to fall ... like any living body when it falls down dead.

Like any dead body when it falls and cannot rise.

[*Resigned*] That means it's time for Him to show himself to me.

[*Terrified*] God, I'm up here on high, happy, here on high, where You usually float. I made smoke for You with all my might, mount on it and show Yourself to me ... Look, I come before You and say:

      – I want to talk to You.

And You answer:

      – Talk!

[*Almost crying*] Now I'm asking:

      – How are You, God?

How are You? Because You have a million old icons, beautifully painted by skilled masters, which show You in a million forms. Now a mountain, now water, now bread. And I've come to see You only in one. And I have started from the bottom upwards. I prayed to every stone, every Saint, I believed in everything, in niches and recesses and in the cracks of stone slabs. I breathed my soul on every wall so that I might climb to there.

The upper part of the body has disappeared into the hollow of the vaulted dome.

God, I've come to thank You for the smoke.

[*Long silence*] Now ... I think I'd like to return ... Maybe someone else has found his way here ... You know, he mustn't believe that even the Verger ... Only ... where have they disappeared to? I had scraped together some scaffolding ... scaffolding ... I couldn't climb the walls ... And look, I step downwards ... [*Terrified*] and soar upwards! And You can't

46

even be seen . . . outside of me . . . Because there's no one higher than me. And I float, God, on clouds like You.
[*With revelation*] I can't fall anymore, just like You. The world is on the right and on the left. And I am in the middle . . .
[*Understanding*] Then . . .
[*Calls*] I!
[*Crying*] Then . . . I'm sorry for myself as well. [*Pause*]
And this candle end . . . I want to see if it's still good for something . . .
[*Sets alight to his clothes*] I'll let it burn . . . to the end . . . for my soul . . . that's all . . .

Above there is only a stake visible, throwing fantastic lights over the black cathedral.

That's all . . . for my . . . soul.

CURTAIN

The Verger: Romanian production, 1981.

TSM-E

The Matrix: Romanian production, 1980.

THE MATRIX

A two-act play in six scenes

CHARACTERS

IRINA, the future mother, 23 years old

OLD MAN, Irina's father

FIRST BEING
SECOND BEING   Three masks present at the vigil,
THIRD BEING   if necessary – Fates

THE VOICE (young man)

Act 1 Scene 1

Rain. Thunder, lightning, wind. A slithery country road. Many a tree torn from its roots blocks the path. A primeval setting from any props the theatre possesses. IRINA, *going towards home, seems the only woman in the world, or the last pregnant woman, whose shoulders are weighed down with the great responsibility of continuity. Her homeward footsteps are immediately obliterated by mud; this frightens her: she leaves no trace. It seems to have been raining since the world began.*

IRINA: [*She runs carefree, hair and clothes wet, somehow revelling in a shared natural event. She shelters under a tree.*]: So wet! It makes your mouth water. Your mouth is full of clouds and when it thunders your teeth chatter . . . and their enamel cracks . . . This extraordinary storm must have pulled out so many . . . We'll have to hang on tight to our wisdom teeth . . . [*Looking around her*] How I long for a dry word. [*Searching*] 'The Flood' . . . [*Laughs. Imitating a storyteller*] "It hadn't dried up after the first flood, beds of seas and oceans were still hazing mirrors, when the devil this time decided to unleash the second deluge. First, to act as kin to the other, and second, because the world had become too holy . . . " Perhaps that's how a future Bible will tell the story. [*She laughs, revealing her white teeth*] It's a good thing to laugh in a storm, your teeth shine if they're beautiful. It's good to laugh in a storm if you've got good teeth . . . Oh, how childish I am [*A little angry at herself*] In fact I'm just being wild and silly. [*Softening a little*] A goose . . . a wild goose. [*Seriously*] Something's happening all around me . . . I don't know what on earth's going on, and I . . . it's as if I'm floating on waves, on seas and oceans . . . psst! – Hush! Ssh! Something moved. I heard it with my own ears . . . [*Listens*] [*Shouts*] Who's there? [*Afraid*] Again . . . like that, like a leaf or an eye opening . . . you feel the eyelid. [*She starts back afraid*] Don't move or . . . don't move or I'll shoot [*Imitates a hunter's movements*] It might be a hare . . . I'll

53

call the hunters . . . [*Loudly*] Hunters, there's something moving over here . . . over here, close by . . . It's as if it's in the earth . . . a mole? . . . I can feel some very . . . very frightened . . . movements . . . of something alive . . . Listen, just then . . . Oh, that frightened me . . . Who on earth . . . takes advantage of this weather like a pig . . . who knows what's brewing . . . the truth is I'm happy . . . yes, that's the word. I feel a strange happiness . . . quite unexplicable . . . of such an extraordinary intensity . . . almost like the time when I was small, forgetful, spoilt, and in my mother's womb . . . Yes, yes, spoilt – but not forgetful. [*Moves her hand impatiently*] Now's not the time for memories. For *such* memories . . . But I can't explain my feelings . . . very similar to . . . anyway . . . it's not important! Let's get home. It's getting dark. I mean the sky's electricity is running out. [*Lightning flash*] Look, it's started to flicker already. [*She sets off, taking a few steps with difficulty. A huge oak tree with a large hollow appears before her. A hollow in which one can sit quite comfortably. Studying the opening.*] From this tree . . . a coffin's just flown away, flown in time to leave just the right amount of space . . . for life's abundance. [*Laughs and only now can it be seen that she's pregnant. She inclines her ear as if trying to listen to her womb.*] Who are you in there? [*Laughs and carefully gets into the space. Enacting humorously.*] If this is the flood . . . please enter the ark. [*Holding out her hand*] It's still raining. It hasn't stopped yet. I was worried that once I'd got in here the phenomenon would change its course . . . and leave me to float on dry land like this. [*Holds out her other hand*] Oh, God, what rain! [*Thoughtfully*] Maybe it'll never stop. [*Nestling into the hollow*] Now we've time to consider a little philosophy. Idealistic inside – materialistic outside . . . [*Laughing, she shivers with the cold*] Really, what luck to find this hollow! Is that what they call . . . now how does that saying go? "In Mother Nature's bosom". [*Sadly*] No, I was in Mother Nature then . . . in mother's womb . . . Now, I'm in an old hollow from which something has just flown . . . [*Remembering*] Everything was like a sweet light . . . which I ate . . . with the tips of my toes . . . and fingers, and all my skin . . . I was floating . . . [*Sadly*] I haven't floated since then . . . Since then I haven't floated . . . nor eaten light . . . with my elbow or with both knees . . . Nor have I flown easily through infinite space. I haven't . . . [*Laughing*] I think I'm the only one in the world . . . any way the only one in the village . . . well at any rate

the only one in this hollow tree . . . who has memories . . . from a
mother's womb . . . [*Prosaically*] That's what's strange about
me . . . I even told my husband, before we married: "You see I
have visions from before . . . " He said, "Do you have them
often?"
"No, don't worry, they're not what you think . . . sometimes . . . I
can't explain it, but when it's quiet . . . Or when it's raining . . . "
[*Laughs*] He says I'm playing make-believe while everything
around me is advancing constructively! As if imagination isn't
also constructive energy. He says "Intra-uterine pamperings, dear.
It's about time you grew up . . . grow up with the times" [*Laughs*]
And look how I grew! I grew up and so did my tummy . . . It's
incredible how grown up it's become . . . it's raining again and all
sorts of pranks spring to mind . . . things that have actually
happened . . . that I've lived . . . [*Sadly*] How intensely I lived
before I was born . . . That's why I'm afraid . . . of ageing too fast,
wearing out, if perhaps, there were too many excesses . . . there in
heaven . . . [*Loud and clear*] I've been to heaven . . . We all come
from there . . . On foot . . . Crawling . . . [*Hugging the tree's
hollow*] Mother! Mother! No: Mother Nature! How beautiful to
be in your house when it's raining . . . [*Dryly*] But I'll have to
leave you to get home. Home, sweet home . . . Let's rest here just
a little longer, and then we'll set off walking through this deluge.
[*For a time she listens to the rain*] I think the happiness which
came over me just now wasn't mine but his . . . [*She strokes her
large round womb, which she can almost feel breathing under the
wet clothes.*] I'm flooded with his happiness . . . that's why I feel
so well . . . [*Lightning and thunder*] What does it matter if the
deluge has begun? What does it matter that the dam's about to
burst . . . Everyone's at the river . . . at the dam . . . I laid a brick
as well . . . [*Thunder and lightning*] Actually it was cow dung, the
first thing I could lay my hands on. People wouldn't let me lift
anything else . . . They all nagged me to, "Go back home. We'll
manage . . . There's plenty of people who can build . . . You've
got another mission . . . " As if giving birth was a mission . . .
They're strange, those peasants . . . Maybe my mission was to
stay there on the wave of earth and stones . . . to fight the floods
. . . [*In a different tone*] Anyway, exercise is supposed to help
birth . . . I've certainly had a lot of it today. If I had to give birth
today . . . [*Sadly*] it'd be the end of happiness for him who's going
to be my son, and I'd be sad, very sad . . . distressed! [*Concen-*

trating as if in a trance] Then . . . a few days before it happened I felt something . . . in fact I was measuring time by other means, perhaps with my eyelashes on mother's womb, notching as on a tally. I felt that something was happening . . . something; like an illness . . . [*Shudders*] unknown until that very moment . . . [*Terrified*] They were the shudders of death! Because until then I had been immortal . . . Something seemed to be circling me . . . I lost the ability to float free in space . . . I was falling . . . falling . . . falling . . . and suddenly disaster struck . . . total collapse . . . [*Sighing*] They say it was a difficult birth for my mother . . . Yes, I remember it clearly, that catastrophe , . . Maybe instinctively I fought against it . . . I was used to heaven . . . and immortality . . . What rubbish! As my husband would say, "Intra-uterine nonsense, dear!" But here, in this hollow tree I can talk quite openly . . . [*Smiling*] Nature is also a mother and understands . . . the situation . . . [*In a different tone*] I saw myself just now in a drop of rain by a flash of lightning. [*With sadness*] I'm not beautiful any more – and it's a pity. A woman should be beautiful until the very last moment . . . My dying father will see me in this sorry state and die with a bad impression of the world . . . The boy, when he first opens his eyes will just see a hag that frightens him . . . yet I'm not that frightening . . . Until quite recently men would turn their heads to look at me . . . all except my own man . . . who turns his head to look at others! . . . At least that's what I think because I've not actually seen him do it . . . And now he's fighting the waves . . . I begged him not to go too far out in his boat . . . He knows it won't be long now and the state father's in . . . poor, poor father . . . If he hadn't been so ill, I would have stayed longer at the dam. But things are so desperate . . . except him . . . [*She feels a contraction and puts her hand to her abdomen*] God! How everything suddenly happens at once! I can feel him getting restless . . . eager to come into the world, to have a purpose . . . a destiny . . . It's as if he's struggling and turning face to his wall . . . not wanting to die . . . [*Explaining*] Now I'm talking about father . . . until then it was the baby . . . Good God, am I mixing them up? Such pains have started . . . I seem to be losing track of what I'm saying . . . no, they've gone again . . . But I'd better move from here, even though it is nice and warm. Anyway, we have a tub I can get into . . . no, a roof above which might be the tub . . . where worries await us . . . let's look outside again . . . [*Looking*] It makes you shiver. [*Bravely*] The rain seems never-ending. Thousands of gutters implanted in clouds. Our village found itself under such a gutter which runs on and on and on. The hooves of cattle have softened. Cows' udders have thinned with the water. Clouds are so low, that wild geese wanting to rise above, swim through them, but drown. The depth of a cloud is ten kilometres . . . You slip at every step . . . Is the earth sliding downwards? I must look after my breasts in case water gets into the milk. That's all we'd need. I can tell that his first worry is going to be . . . the food supply. [*Examining herself anxiously*] What if I've not got enough milk? They could be only for show, just a matter of form! [*Laughs*] I once heard a woman complaining that she'd no *bust*. How stupid I am! [*She hesitates to go out but then plucks up courage. Outside, the rain is still drumming. She takes shelter near another tree. A flash of lightning. The oak tree with the hollow burns like a candle. She watches the flames.*] Unbelievable! . . . It waited for me to leave before setting itself on fire . . . or letting itself be struck by lightning . . . and so pass into oblivion. Such huge candles – who are they lit for? [*With certainty*] All this fury in vain . . . Nothing can touch me . . . as long as this job remains to be finished . . . There exists a unity between things which once started have to be finished . . . a unity of pregnant things . . . If I was still in the hollow . . . the lightning would have avoided us. Yes, oh yes, I'm sure of that. [*Caressing her abdomen*] Come on, little one . . . [*Loudly, above the noise of the storm*] Unity of all things about to give birth . . . help me! [*Thunder, lightning. Irina begins to leave, slipping on the mud*]

CURTAIN

Act 1 Scene 2

The interior of a peasant's house. Two differently furnished rooms, one for the young couple, the other for the deathbed. Between them there is an entrance hall leading to the outside. The doors of the two rooms are wide open. One can see into both. In the one on the right, IRINA, crouched in bed, pale, her forehead covered in sweat, is in the throes of childbirth. On the left, the OLD MAN, Irina's father, goes through the agony of dying. He is dying a natural death, so he is not concerned. Natural death, like an easy delivery . . .

He has asked for his coffin, which he had prepared beforehand, to be brought closer to him. The Old Man and Irina converse, each from their own room, each from their own beds of suffering.

OLD MAN: It's starting to smell . . .

IRINA: What is?

OLD MAN: This throne . . . Only yesterday it smelt fine, an oak smell it was . . . and now it reeks of resin . . . Do you reckon someone's changed it?

IRINA [*in great pain*]: What are you going on about? Who on earth could have changed it?

OLD MAN: I'm sure I ordered an oak one . . . it were oak, until yesterday . . . until a minute ago . . . [*With determination*] You'll only get me into a pine one over my . . .

IRINA: Stop thinking about it . . .

OLD MAN: What should I think of then . . . Women?

IRINA: Yes, [*Trying to smile*] women.

OLD MAN: There is one that keeps prowling around here . . . the one with the scythe . . .

IRINA: I told you to stop thinking about it . . .

OLD MAN: Why, she's a woman too isn't she? She might even be a virgin. I think the smells got mixed up. It were stored with the pine ones . . . and the healthy . . . moist smell of the oak coffin spread to the others, two a penny . . . which only lasts you to the grave . . . and sometimes not as far as that . . . I once heard of a man who fell out of his . . . and woke up . . . 'cos he weren't quite dead . . . just as they were about to bury him . . . otherwise . . .

IRINA: Otherwise what?

OLD MAN: The smell of resin got into mine . . .

IRINA: Ah!

OLD MAN: 'Cos look [*He gasps for breath*] . . . I can't even breathe now . . . 'cos of that resin . . .

IRINA: It's the air, the fresh air . . .

OLD MAN: What, from the coffin?

IRINA: Why don't you admit you don't feel like dying . . . Why did you ask them to bring that thing here for anyway, right under your nose?

OLD MAN [*gets up and goes to sit on the coffin*]: That's why . . .

IRINA: Well, why?

OLD MAN: So no one could change it . . . but I still think . . . [*He examines the lid*] Ah, to hell with it . . . I think it's all right . . . [*In a different tone*] Don't rush to put me under . . . call a doctor from the town to feel my pulse . . . when I'm dead . . . 'cos that's all they are good for . . . and when he says, "He's a gonner," . . . you be sure and wait three more days . . . for you can never tell . . . and if I don't blink an eyelid . . . then that's that . . . But during that time give me full honours, mind . . . you know what I mean . . . I want all the customs. Mourn well for me! Have a good wail! . . .

IRINA [*to reassure him*]: You've got a long time to go yet . . .

OLD MAN: You mean: We'll think about that when the time comes . . . [*Laughs hollowly*]

IRINA: Father, what do you mean? . . . Who do you think wants you to die?

OLD MAN: Her with the scythe . . .

IRINA: Are you still in pain?

OLD MAN: I never felt pain in my life, except here in my soul . . . I don't know what's up with me . . .

IRINA: The doctors said there was nothing up with you . . .

OLD MAN: Well if there's nothing up with me at my age . . . it must be bad. Real bad. [*He gets up, rummages through a chest and gets out some clothes*]

IRINA: Now what are you doing?

OLD MAN: Nothing. I'm just getting dressed up.

IRINA: Why, where are you going?

OLD MAN: I know where I'm going . . . [*Dresses with difficulty*] Not even my Sunday Best looks right any more . . . If there were still time I'd go to the tailor and have him alter it a bit . . . [*Laughs*]

IRINA: I never know when you're joking and when you're being serious . . . Even now I sense you're up to something.

OLD MAN: I wouldn't mind if I was . . . but the thing is . . . Just look at that!

IRINA [*alarmed*]: What?

OLD MAN: I've got one sock on inside out . . . and I haven't got the strength to start all over again . . . I wonder if . . . they'll have me at the Last Judgement looking like this? Do you think they'll pick on me? They might start poking fun . . . [*Lies down on the bed, groaning as he does so.*] It's not bad being dressed up for death . . . it's one thing less to worry about . . . In fact it's two: the worry of the hereafter as well.

IRINA [*attempting to change the subject*]: Just listen to that rain outside . . .

OLD MAN: I wish the flood would come . . . though perhaps better not . . . it's not right for it to rain like this. Runny dung don't need much rain. Maybe it's that that's shortened my life . . .

IRINA [*sighs, groans*]: You'll live longer than me!

OLD MAN [*following a line of thought*]: As I was saying, when someone's ready to go, it's the mind that goes first . . . mine's still clear . . .

IRINA: You've enough for everyone . . .

OLD MAN: If only I had some strength as well . . . look, I can only just manage to do up my shirt. But what are you doing in there? Aren't you going to come and hold my candle?

IRINA: Are you really dying?

OLD MAN: I could be.

IRINA [*trying to get up, but the pain pulls her down again*]: So that's how one dies . . . like you . . . healthy . . . and with all your wits about you . . . joking?

OLD MAN: Life was a joke . . . This is . . . serious . . . [*Looking for something*] Now where could your mother have put my cap?

IRINA: Haven't you worn it since *then*? That's nearly five years ago . . .

OLD MAN: That's right, about five years ago, 'Cos she hurried on.

IRINA: I don't know . . . and I haven't the energy to go and look for it.

OLD MAN: Oh, leave it then . . . Anyway, I'd have only held it in my hand . . . They say you're not allowed to wear your cap in heaven or in hell . . . In hell 'cos it's too hot and up there . . . 'cos it's not allowed . . . There are only Saints there . . . Sometimes I close my eyes . . . and I feel quite dizzy. It's as if I can see them, groups of them, spreading the mystery. Have you remembered?

IRINA: What?

OLD MAN: Where she could have put it?

IRINA [*her thoughts miles away*]: What?

OLD MAN: My cap!

IRINA: Wait a bit, Dad . . . then I'll get up and look for you . . . but look . . . Now it's cutting into me again [*Sighs and groans*] Oh, God!

OLD MAN [*after a time*]: Are you mourning me?

IRINA: It's coming on again . . .

OLD MAN: That's good . . .

IRINA [*shrieking out*]: It's agony . . . agony . . . How can it be good?

OLD MAN: Because there'll be another here instead of me. And the house won't be empty after we've gone . . . Just you make sure it's a boy now.

IRINA [*just about managing a joke*]: It's too dark. I can't see anything. It could be a girl, because even my sight's gone blurred . . .

OLD MAN [*in a weak voice*]: What do you think? Have you long to go? You hurry up there now, 'cos if I knew it would be over quickly I'd wait a bit longer.

IRINA [*cheerfully*]: Oh, Dad, it's good to have you near just now. You make me laugh so I forget a little . . .

OLD MAN: I'd come to help you . . . I know how your poor mother suffered having you . . . but, first I'd be too embarrassed . . . and second, my legs have gone all numb . . . they're like logs now. Cold as ice as well . . .

IRINA: It's like a fire in my womb . . .

OLD MAN: Shall we change over? [*He laughs*]

IRINA: If it was up to me . . . [*Cries out very loudly*] . . . I'm dying . . .

OLD MAN: Hey! What's all this noise? You're not dying . . . But it's harder for you 'cos you've got an education . . . that's why it feels so funny . . . Your grandmother went bringing food to the fields and on her way back she brought the baby with her in the basket. She brought it on her head, in the basket with the pots and pans . . . She had it in the shade of some undergrowth, wherever she happened to be . . . had it quickly in some bush just like the animals. That's how she had fourteen . . . I was the thirteenth . . .

IRINA: Unlucky number! [*Groans*]

OLD MAN: I was always the thirteenth . . . That's why I'm going . . . [*Groans*] That's why I'm kicking the bucket now. [*Groans*] Have you long to go?

IRINA: [*Groans*]

OLD MAN: That's it. Hurry up then. [*Groans*]

61

IRINA: I'm sorry for you . . .

OLD MAN: You'd better let the midwife know . . . In fact it's me who ought to go. But how can I? Oh, the pain under my ribs . . .

IRINA: [*Screams*]

OLD MAN: You see? It would have been better if we'd not sent you to school . . . you'd have had it with no pains at all . . . just like simple folk. Your mother only went to infant school . . . and she only just managed to have you . . . you went higher . . . So you'll see how hard you'll find it . . . You'll even need a midwife . . . Has our village got a midwife?

IRINA: [*Groans*] Yes, yes it has . . . but what's schooling got to do with . . . this?

OLD MAN: Oh it has . . . It weakens . . . the gums . . . I told you about your grandmother . . . fourteen and didn't even know how to count them . . . [*Laughs*] They were healthier times!

IRINA: [*Moans*]

OLD MAN: Well . . . yes . . . if the hens found it that hard to lay eggs, what wailing then there'd be in the courtyard . . .

IRINA: Perhaps they don't cluck for pleasure. Yet I can't wait to cluck for pleasure . . . [*Pauses*]

OLD MAN: What's happening now?

IRINA: Don't make me laugh . . . or I'll drop it . . . I mustn't force it. [*Groans*] What's it like to die?

OLD MAN: Nothing special. You just go out, like a candle.

IRINA: Ehhh!

OLD MAN: I hope we've got more candles. This one's nearly finished and I'm still here!

IRINA: What are you doing? Holding your own candle?

OLD MAN: Well, if I haven't got any children . . . ready to jump up and do it. [*Sadly*] Now you listen to me, it's no use having them . . .

IRINA: Well . . .

OLD MAN: Rather than die like a heathen without a candle, better to . . . Eh! Do you know I've not confessed yet?

IRINA: You should have thought about it before now . . . Why didn't you do it when you ordered the coffin?

OLD MAN: What shall I tell the priest? I talk and he's miles away, thinking of the funeral supper and anything else that might be on his mind. But now I'd like to confess. Who can I get to go and fetch him?

IRINA [*smiling*]: If you wait a bit longer, we can send . . . the little one . . .

OLD MAN: That's the problem. I can't wait much longer. Will you hear me?

IRINA: I'll hear you, but I'm no priest . . .

OLD MAN: It doesn't matter, you're my daughter . . . much purer than a priest . . . Listen, Lass, [*Silence*] I don't know how to begin.

IRINA: The candles are there, at the head of the bed . . . Can you turn round?

OLD MAN: I can turn . . . but not from the grave . . . because no one returns from there . . . [*Looking for the candles*] It's all right, I'll manage . . . You get on with your job . . . Hurry up, mind . . . Make sure nothing's twisted. Do you hear me?

IRINA: Yes, I can hear you.

OLD MAN: How did I live as long as this?

IRINA: How?

OLD MAN: It's like drinking holy water, it doesn't quench the thirst or stifle the hunger . . . and you don't even become a Saint . . . [*Bitterly*] That's how I've lived. I didn't understand much . . . we simply lived . . . We never think about life until the final hour.

IRINA [*turning it into a joke*]: – and then only for a quarter of an hour.

OLD MAN [*seriously*]: 'Cos someone . . . comes . . . beckoning to us . . . scowling at us . . . saying, "Faster! Faster! Get a move on." And when she tells you to move, you stop dead. Aye! That's how it is in the countryside, always following the sun and the seasons . . . and there's always something to be done . . . You know what? If I die, bury me in the town! There I know I'll have a rest . . . Yet, best not! They might set the alarm ringing next to my head . . . It's lucky the sun doesn't ring when it rises.

IRINA: [*Laughs*]

OLD MAN: Aye, my girl . . . what has been, has been . . . And it's been good! But it's caught me a bit unprepared now, and that's why I'm sorry . . . I had the coffin made in time . . . but look I haven't strength left to get into it . . . Because it's taken me unawares . . . [*Makes efforts to get into the coffin*]

IRINA [*irritated*]: Stay still . . . What are you trying to get into? Why are you so restless? It's as if you are turning inside me . . .

OLD MAN: Perhaps I've never been born . . . How right you are. Then I'd get another chance, wouldn't I? [*Laughs with difficulty*] Forgive me, God. Is it hurting bad, Lass?

IRINA: Very bad.

OLD MAN [*afraid*]: Then . . . who shall I confess to . . . for there's a song I'd wail even to the stones?

IRINA [*taking her part seriously*]: Tell me what's on your mind . . . but be quick . . . 'cos I might go before you do . . . Have you sinned much?

OLD MAN: Never! . . . I didn't have enough time for that . . . I could have been happier . . . but it weren't to be. Your mother were the same . . . How could she have left me alone to go on suffering? [*Heavy silence, interrupted by groans from either one side or the other*]

For a time Irina forgets about the sick man, consumed by her own physical pain. She talks to herself . . . like the Old Man. For a few moments their lines don't meet. They no longer answer each other . . . being merely fragments of monologue.

OLD MAN [*groaning*]: Have you heard of Doctor Paicu?

IRINA: No . . . Was he a woman's doctor?

OLD MAN: No, no, he looked at lungs. But he got cancer . . . A month before dying, he announced the exact day and hour he'd die. Exactly! And he were right. On the day he'd said, at nearly eleven o'clock, he rang his best friend . . . It'll soon strike eleven, he said. Aren't you coming over . . . to have a chat?

IRINA [*complaining*]: Oh, God, God!

OLD MAN: So he came, they talked for a while . . .

IRINA: What about?

OLD MAN: Oh, this and that, as men do. And when the clock were ready to strike, because he had one of those clocks . . . which struck its chest with pride . . . he looked at it and said, "Now it's over, I'm going."

IRINA [*loosing the thread*]: Well, didn't his friend come to him? Where did the sick man say he was going?

OLD MAN [*continuing*]: That's what drove them all mad . . . the doctors, his friends from the hospitals . . . they all realised that because this Paicu had foreseen it all so clearly, he must have also found the cure.

IRINA: What cure?

OLD MAN [*slightly irritated*]: Can't you spare me a bit of your time?

IRINA: I'm in terrible pain . . .

OLD MAN: . . . He'd found the cure for cancer . . . and he took the secret with him, because he'd quarrelled with them he worked with.

IRINA [*shrieking*]: Stop going on about death!

OLD MAN: Quiet. You stop going on about birth.

IRINA [*after a pause*]: Round about New Year, people seem to love each other a little more . . . have you noticed?

OLD MAN [*grumpily*]: No.

IRINA: Last year I came across a man I once exchanged two or three words with and I'd forgotten him . . . he looked intensely at me, took my hand and said: "Come, there's still time to catch this year." [*Laughing*] Just like that, out of the blue!

OLD MAN: Were he mad?

IRINA: No . . . I don't think so . . .

OLD MAN: Did you slap him?

IRINA: Yes, but his expression of despair stayed fixed in my mind . . . it was that of a drowning man . . . and . . . I know! "Come on let's still try to make something of this year."

OLD MAN: A good-for-nothing.

IRINA: No, because . . . what were you thinking? He didn't want much. He'd just come to the village with his waggon . . . and wanted to take me to the pictures . . . You know, so he could boast that he'd seen a film with me . . . in the year that had just gone, or anyway, that he'd done something in the year that had passed . . . some kind of activity . . .

OLD MAN: I'd like to make something of the year that's coming . . . [*Laughs*] But all my bones hurt.

IRINA: They never hurt you before . . .

OLD MAN: Before it were my flesh that hurt and now it's only the bones . . . the pain seems to have separated . . . as it says in the Bible . . .

IRINA: Where does it say that?

OLD MAN: The water will separate from the land . . . [*After a pause, sighing*] Why haven't I got cancer?

IRINA: God didn't choose you.

OLD MAN: At least I'd have know what I were dying from . . . I'd have been at peace, even proud dying of an important illness, one without a cure . . . 'cos I've even said to the health people: "Now that I'm going, I'd like to know . . . Now tell me . . . I've got cancer, haven't I?" "No," one of them said, "Then what have I got?" And he says, "I don't know . . . Nothing seems to be wrong with you." [*As if in revolt*] Why is all your education silent when faced with death?

IRINA: Why my education?

TSM-F

65

OLD MAN: Yours, because I sent you to school . . . You're a teacher . . . Yours, the scholars', the doctors'. That fellow, why did he say "I don't know"?

IRINA: He wasn't a doctor, he was a vet.

OLD MAN: What's the difference? They all know just as much . . . Only that Paicu might have unearthed something . . . but had already fallen out with his workmates . . . Pity! I heard all about it, when coming in the cart. They were all sorry for him.

IRINA: Now if there was someone about to get him, it would still be the vet who'd come . . .

OLD MAN: How this life passes! [*Sighs*]

IRINA: The other one's coming . . .

OLD MAN: It's arleady come . . . it's under the bed.

IRINA: Maybe under my bed, but I can't look . . .

OLD MAN: In your belly. [*Laughs*]

IRINA: Some people loose their heads . . . with just a cold . . . They can't even put two words together any more. They get panic-stricken, and you, father . . . who could believe that . . . if anyone was to hear you and couldn't see you in that throne, if they could hear you talking such nonsense, they'd think you were playing a part . . . or getting ready for a wedding.

OLD MAN: Well, let's call it a wedding . . . if we can't call it nothing else. Who knows . . . maybe that's why I have got dressed up like this.

IRINA: You've always laughed at danger . . .

OLD MAN: 'Cos there's not much else you can do. I saw a man at the Front . . . A shell had smashed him to pieces, and he still had a smile on his face . . . Only one lip were on one side and the other was about ten metres away . . . He was saying something dead hilarious . . . but you couldn't make it out very well. Grass had begun to grow through his laugh. [*Pauses*] I wonder how many years it is since I died?

IRINA: Are you asking me?

OLD MAN: Well, I'm not talking to myself.

IRINA: I don't talk to ghosts.

OLD MAN [*sighing*]: It's as if I'd been gone . . . for about a hundred years . . . One hundred . . . coins . . . I mean years . . . My speech is slurred . . . [*Frightened*] Have I been wandering?

IRINA: A little bit. You thought you'd been dead a long time . . .

OLD MAN: How do we know it's not like that? Can you put the light on, so I can have a look . . .

IRINA: I can't . . .

OLD MAN: See? [*Pauses*] I was thinking of Rita . . . your mother . . . it seems like a hundred years . . . since . . . one hundred years . . . half a sovereign . . .

IRINA [*afraid*]: Father!

OLD MAN: What's she saying?

IRINA: Who's saying? You're not talking sense any more.

OLD MAN: It's finished . . . it's gone . . . I felt so weak . . . Will it pass the same afterwards?

IRINA: What?

OLD MAN: Time . . . just as fast? . . .

IRINA: Ah! How should I know?

OLD MAN: My strength went all of a sudden . . . Have you got long to go?

IRINA [*determined*]: I've changed my mind. I'll miscarry. [*Shouting*] I don't want to . . . I don't want to . . . give birth any more. [*Softly*] What use will be be anyway? It's terrible to live as you've lived . . . wars, poverty, drought, people falling dead – to the right and left of you.

OLD MAN [*bitterly*]: So what! You can't disown them. They're your own dead. Don't start judging me . . . or I'll get out of . . . and come to you . . . and give you what for . . . 'cos I'm not dead yet . . . How dare you judge me, you . . . [*Coughing fit*] Fancy that!

IRINA: I don't want to! [*Noises, thuds are heard in the woman's room*]

OLD MAN [*after a pause, listening to the noises*]: Are you having it now?

IRINA [*angrily*]: No! I'm killing it. [*Shouts*] I don't want to bring anyone into this world any more . . . I can't . . . Better to kill it in the womb . . . It's better for him . . . He can't feel anything . . . It's like treading on a leaf . . . it doesn't hurt it . . . and you rid it of winter's frosts. [*Cries*]

OLD MAN: If you cry it means you're sorry for what you were going to do . . . Those are the airs and graces of a lady . . . If you were a peasant woman you wouldn't have got into such a tantrum . . . There now, at school they turned you into a lady . . . Everything that comes from God must have life . . .

IRINA: Then you, why should you die?

OLD MAN: I've lived long enough . . . Oh, much too long. I can't live a whole century. That's what poor old Cornea used to say! And he lived a century and a half. He could eat a whole sheep for a meal . . . and he slept, summer or winter, outside on the porch.

IRINA: When he said he wouldn't live a century, he was probably thinking of his second century.

OLD MAN: Quite! He had grandchildren, great grandchildren and great-great grandchildren. He were like an oak tree left in a clearing waiting for the lightning to strike it down . . . The whole village knew him only as an old man . . . For about a hundred years he'd been called 'Old Man' [*Sighing*] I've been called 'Old Man' a long time too, and I don't even know if I'll live to become a grandfather . . . [*With hope*] Will I live to be a grandfather:

IRINA [*sadly*]: I don't know . . . I'm afraid he's dead . . . He doesn't seem to move anymore . . . [*Afraid*] What if he's dead? I hit him quite hard . . .

OLD MAN: Well as long as you hit him on his bottom? [*With certainty*] He won't come to no harm. A mother's beating is like a stranger's caress.

IRINA: He's moved again. He's living. [*Endearingly*] My little one . . .

OLD MAN: I'd like you to christen him . . . like his grandfather . . . Ion!

IRINA: Ah, no. Not that . . . Another Ion? Better Stan . . .

OLD MAN: I don't like that name . . . I remember someone called Stan who grazed goats all his life . . . Better Gheorge, like Bazavan . . .

IRINA: I don't want to call him that.

OLD MAN: Vasile?

IRINA: It's too much towards the end of the alphabet . . . everybody would be in front of him . . .

OLD MAN [*irritated*]: Anyway . . . just don't give him any of those fancy foreign names or I'll curse him to hell . . . I'll disown him as a grandson. Don't ruin the boy's name! [*Pause. Noises come from the sick man's room*]

IRINA: What are you up to in there? What are you rattling about? [*Noises*] Hey, what's going on? A moment ago you had no strength left! What are you knocking over?

OLD MAN: Nothing . . . I've got in the box at last . . . into the ship . . . I've climbed into Noah's Ark . . .

IRINA: Are you in the mood for joking?

OLD MAN: It seems warm in here . . . I were feeling a bit cold . . . It's warmer here.

IRINA: Well anyway, does it fit you?

OLD MAN: No, it's a bit tight here . . . under a rib . . . [*Laughs*]

IRINA: Tight?

OLD MAN: Under a rib . . . on the other side . . . I won't get very far in this boat either . . .

IRINA: It's not as if you're going anywhere!

OLD MAN: That's true. As long as a man's young . . . he likes to go round the world . . . and when her with the scythe scowls at him . . . he'd hide even down a snake's hole . . . just like a dog, when it's going to die . . . comes to the doorstep . . . and dies faithfully . . . on the threshold . . . where his master can see it . . . at least he believes in his master . . . But we . . . who are we to believe in?

IRINA: The threshold . . .

OLD MAN: How right you are . . . Now I'm on the threshold . . . but I can't die until I see Him . . . Do you hear?

IRINA: What?

OLD MAN: You know what the custom is around here? . . . They'll come for the vigil.

IRINA: What for?

OLD MAN: To keep vigil for me . . . that's what it's called. To stay with the dead during the first night . . . when his soul is still in the house . . . and their duty is to entertain him . . . so that he don't feel lonely. That's the custom . . . They're a bit loud mouthed . . . and use foul language . . . 'cos you don't know them . . . They get dressed up like hell . . . and babble on . . . But don't get upset . . . I've done many vigils . . . It's even quite pleasant . . . and for the relatives . . . because you make them laugh . . . They forget a little. Someone dies, but that don't mean the end of the world . . . The living must have some fun . . . They mustn't catch the grief . . . The living must live their lives . . . [*In a different tone*] Now I feel a bit thirsty.

IRINA: Thirsty?

OLD MAN: Thirsty. But I can't get out again . . . Better to stay here . . . I've only just got warm. Is it still raining outside?

IRINA [*listens*]: Still . . .

OLD MAN: Why bother to get out! . . . For a drop of water . . . Anyway, I'm more sheltered here . . . But I don't know why my mouth keeps going so dry . . . I can't even turn . . . I'm pegging out here . . . I've closed my account with life . . . drawn a line . . . and laid below it . . . I'm off and leaving you. And tell your man not to beat you.

IRINA: Why should he?

OLD MAN: If he don't look like him . . .

IRINA [*laughing*]: Then whom should be look like?

OLD MAN [*afraid*]: But who's cut down that oak tree in front of the house? I don't remember seeing it lately.

IRINA: How could you have seen it if you're lying in it? . . . Didn't you say you wanted it made from oak . . . ? [*Pause*]

OLD MAN: Have the herons gone?

IRINA: Yes, gone.

OLD MAN: And the sprouts? Have they flown as well to warmer parts?

IRINA: Maybe the storks . . . because we've put the sprouts in the barrel . . .

OLD MAN: Yes . . . yes . . . in the warm barrels . . . I don't know why . . . Or who we were talking about. My jaws are setting . . . I can hardly . . . shout . . . [*Shouts*]

IRINA: Why did I cry out so loudly . . . I don't think it hurt that much . . . like now . . . it's as if it's not even my voice . . .

OLD MAN [*shouting*]: God . . . Oh, God!

IRINA [*shouting*]: God . . . Oh, God!

The screams and groans intensify in both rooms. Darkness

IRINA: Do I hear right? He's started to fight there . . . to shout . . . [*Listening*] Something's in me tearing . . . ah . . . Ssh! He's started talking again.

OLD MAN: A staff and a rod! Give me a staff to hold on to . . . anything. How the sky moves . . . Why haven't you put chains near the precipice? I'm falling! . . . A rope! . . . Quickly throw me a rope . . . to hold onto . . . Such a vast emptiness . . .

IRINA [*shouting to the Old Man*]: Stop crumpling that candle, it's not a rope. The pains are coming on again . . . Ah, I'm dying . . . I shall die first . . .

OLD MAN: Who is it throwing me out of the window? From this height . . . Sacks thrown from the window from one store room to another. From one world to another . . . Better leave me here to rot . . . with the rates who sniff at me with their whiskers . . . Oh, I'm falling! And I said I wasn't afraid . . . I'm frightened to death . . . As if I was being born again. But why? Why . . . am I falling? I didn't know such emptiness existed . . . that there was such a big empty space between . . . clouds . . . between sky and . . . us! The rope . . . ah, I could still catch it! At least for a moment just to get my balance. [*Shouts out*]

IRINA [*listening*]: What a roaring in my womb! . . . A volcano . . . Am I giving birth to a volcano? I catch fire, I'm on fire . . . if only it would end. Do I hear right? They're the words of the one who is to come . . . He is the one who leaves a world . . . How well I know this feeling . . . of collapsing. If only it would end soon . . . Just to end one way or another . . . [*Shouting*] I'm dying! Dying!
OLD MAN [*shouting*]: I'm falling . . . Falling!

CURTAIN

Act 1 Scene 3

The two rooms as in the preceding scene. On the right is the dead one in his coffin holding his own candle in his hand, which is still warm, and will stay so until he reaches heaven, or wherever he ends up. On the left, is the young mother with the swaddled baby. Between the two rooms the door is open. There is a slight draft but the woman is too tired to close it. At the same time she wants to keep an eye on her dead father.

IRINA: I can only feel weariness, and such an emptiness in my head! It's as if I had pulled him from my head, from the brain . . . How strange. Maybe I didn't give birth to a child . . . [*Laughs*] – but only to the idea of a child. [*Didactically*] 'To conceive' is a good term used in connection with procreation . . . in fact it's the only healthy, viable conception. [*Naively*] You bring into the world a small beetle . . . while it rains and thunders in the world. It's good here . . . It only rains when he pees . . . and there's lightning only when the candles seems to be flickering. [*There is a knock at the door*] Ah, help at last. It'll be the people for the Vigil. They'll tend to that side of the house. [*Indicating the room on the right*] Come in! Come in! [*Silence. Then more knocks.*] Hurry in! Make yourself at home!

71

The door opens. At the same time the wind and rain might suggest what waits outside. Three strange masked BEINGS *enter and one cannot tell whether they are men and women.*

IRINA: Welcome ... I was so lonely ... To be honest it's not very pleasant to be in this ... somewhat confused ... situation ... Confused thoughts spring to mind ... I'm telling you because you're from round here, from the village. You must have known me since I was small.

FIRST BEING: Since before you came into the world.

IRINA [*afraid*]: I seem to think that my father died at the exact moment I gave birth ... and at this thought ... suddenly a cold shiver runs down my spine ... Never mind because it's so bad outside and there are many cold shivers around. [*Even more terrified*] It's as if I'd given birth to my father! ... Me, his daughter – to give birth to ... How could that be? It's as if ... [*She wipes the sweat which has appeared on her brow and tries to smile*] ... It's as if I'd given birth to him dead ... I mean with all his life already lived ... with experience of the world ... that is dead without feeling sorry, because, as he used to say, he's lived his days and eaten his maize ... But where? Where has he eaten it?

SECOND BEING: Leave off such nonsense.

IRINA [*bursts into laughter*]: Well done. Well said ... "Nonsense!" Because indeed they're just babblings ... I said them out loud because you know me. I'm quite normal. I think I'd recognise you too if you'd only take off those strange rags, those masks. Who on earth are you, men or women?

THIRD BEING: It was us who came when you were born.

IRINA [*amazed*]: And in that same state? [*Laughs*]

THIRD BEING: What a thing to say!

IRINA [*deep in thought*]: But what were you doing at my birth ... what ... on earth were you doing there? You can't be midwives! I thought you were old men, because poor Father, God rest his soul, told me, he said, you'll see those old men would come dressed fit for hell for the Vigil, but he said you'd make me laugh ... that is, that you'd have a sense of humour ... in the best sense ...

FIRST BEING: These young mothers keep breaking the thread of their thoughts ...

SECOND BEING: Because it's they who remake that link ... [*Leers*]

FIRST BEING: Where is he?

IRINA [*pointing to the dead man*]: Over there . . . What do they call you? You, the one in the middle, seem to be Softy George.

SECOND BEING: Hee! Hee! Hee!

THIRD BEING [*bending over the coffin*]: Charming – boy – Prince Charming –

FIRST BEING: And big . . .

SECOND BEING: Could he weigh four pounds? [*Laughs*]

THIRD BEING: He's well swaddled . . .

FIRST BEING: When you see how quiet he is, you can hardly believe it's him yelling like that . . . as if caught in a serpent's mouth.

SECOND BEING [*incanting a spell*]: He who's come from the serpent's mouth . . . Let him slither like the snake . . . No, snake-like shed his skin . . . No, snake-like hiss from within. No, like a snake let his head be crushed . . . No . . .

FIRST AND THIRD BEING [*protesting*]: Heh! Heh! Don't be so harsh . . .

SECOND BEING [*continuing*]: . . . No, let his body move like a snake No, be wise like a serpent . . . [*Angrily*] . . . No! Now I stammer! . . . [*To the First Being*] You say something better bound!

FIRST BEING: Well-bound like the corn which binds, and his body beautifully bound . . . and the mind unbound . . . and to have fine bonds . . . round his waist a woman's arm . . . At the neck a band because he bound himself with binding vows . . . And the strongest bonds above . . .

SECOND AND THIRD BEINGS [*laughing*]: . . . Up round his neck . . .

FIRST BEING: At the head . . . at the head of a cross . . . little leaves of basil . . .

SECOND BEING: You forgot the bond with earth.

FIRST BEING: That, that's you . . .

IRINA [*puzzled*]: What are you mumbling on about? [*Silence*] They muddle birth with death . . . They mess about . . . instead of telling lewd jokes, as is customary at a vigil . . . They play at being Fates. [*Laughs, shaken with shivers*] But surely Fates should say something a little more uplifting! Whatever they say it will still be lewd . . . since it's about man's destiny. Because . . . compared to the beauty of life seen . . . from the inside . . . just as I saw it a moment before . . . being born . . . truth is pale . . . pale like . . . the dead one . . . God forgive me, like wax . . . like that candle . . . like the wick . . . Yes . . . Yes . . . In my mother's womb I too had a very different view of the world . . . and when I was born,

73

look, there I was giving birth. And at the same time taking part in a vigil.

THIRD BEING: From earth, and grass that's green . . . [*Prancing about the coffin*] From earth, and grass that's green, who is small and can't be seen.

OTHERS: Ha! Ha! Ha!

THIRD BEING: I've seen a sun, ashen rayed and in its shadow old Nastase stayed, black as earth with earth in his bones, and the grass scolded in angry tones . . . why did he return to life, while from his bones wheat sheaves were rife, reaping what he had sown and the sun from earth had grown.

FIRST BEING: Do you mean he's going to be called Nastase?

THIRD BEING: I don't know . . .

FIRST BEING: [*laughing*]: Well, what are you mumbling about then? Don't you know what you're on about?

THIRD BEING: Of course I don't know . . . I am destiny, I'm foretelling . . . predicting . . . words . . . and his fate is to try to link these words . . . one with another . . . to give them . . . exact meaning . . .

SECOND BEING [*laughing*]: Which can be taken either way . . .

THIRD BEING: No, only one way . . . feet first . . .

IRINA [*to herself*]: I'd laugh . . . but I can't cope with it . . . I never believed in fates, spells, witches. There are certain customs . . . which should, I mean . . . if that's the way it's been for generations. [*The child cries*] Oh, what's the matter, love? [*Soothing the child as it cries*]

FIRST BEING: Shhh! We've woken the dead from next door. He'll get angry . . . See, we tend more to the living, and . . . no one stays at the wake with him . . .

SECOND BEING: Freshly dead . . . bad tempered.

THIRD BEING: That's what it's like at first . . . later on when the skin toughens . . .

FIRST BEING [*approaching the coffin*]:Grow healthy and sturdy, grow wings free to cross the sea, and pull a tree to scratch a flea. [*Laughs*]

OTHERS [*to the first*]: Come on, that's enough. Let him sleep . . . to gather strength . . .

THIRD BEING: Go over to the dead man because we've also got a vigil.

FIRST BEING: Not me! I'm either for one or the other.

SECOND BEING [*pleading*]: Only today . . . Once and that's all. [*Child cries again*] Can't you hear him?

THIRD BEING: Be quiet little Tomb . . . We won't be long.

SECOND BEING: I've brought you the sieve and the poker . . . On the poker we put the club and go with you to heaven with a flag. [*Takes the sieve and the poker from under the cloak. All three converge on the child.*]

FIRST BEING [*prancing round Irina and the baby*]: This life . . .

SECOND BEING [*also prancing*]: . . . hereafter . . .

THIRD BEING: . . . which begins on Thursday . . .

SECOND BEING [*choking with laughter*]: . . . and lasts till Doomsday. [*Various movements with the poker and the sieve. They begin to symbolize a kind of enormous phallus above the baby . . . They put the sieve on top and spin it*]

THIRD BEING: If the prop had been any longer he'd have jumped with it over the grave. [*In contortions of laughter*]

SECOND BEING: But as it is . . . he propped it in the grave . . . and it pulled him in . . . [*Clasping hands on belly with laughter*]

IRINA [*confused and lost for words*]: They can't be people from round here, from our village . . . [*Loudly as if to give herself courage before burglars*] Who are you? [*Louder*] Who are you, anyway? Aren't you ashamed? What is this masquerade? [*The Beings continue their game*] Get out!

FIRST BEING [*to the others*]: Sssh! Tip-toe because there are lions here.

IRINA: Deriding the children!

SECOND BEING: A lioness! . . .

IRINA: I shall go to the Mayor. I'll complain about this . . . If my husband was here, he'd show you . . . [*The more furious she becomes the more the Beings are amused*]

FIRST BEING: In this house someone's going to die of laughter . . . [*Clasping hands on belly with laughter*] I can laugh no more.

SECOND BEING: Today everything's worked like magic.

THIRD BEING: And it'll go on working – the deluge has begun . . . What fulfillment . . . filling to the brim. And that's just the beginning.

IRINA [*Grabs a slipper and hits one of the masks. The slipper passes right through the character as if there was nothing there . . . or so it seems to Irina.*]: Oh, my God! I caught him, yet I felt nothing – it's as if I hit air . . . [*Shouts*] Get out! [*The Beings exit in fear*] I'm not sure of the customs. Perhaps I shouldn't have driven them away . . . But they'd gone beyond a joke. I was beginning to feel afraid . . . Even if I don't believe in . . . such stupidity . . . but that's the way it happens. At first you laugh, amusing yourself, then suddenly you're petrified . . . They say that's what happens to the mad . . . In the beginning they *pretend* . . . they're perfectly normal . . . they enjoy the idea of going off their rocker a little, but only of course in the eyes of others . . . when suddenly . . . snap! . . . there they stay . . . These are village folk of course . . . There might even be a woman among them . . . come for the vigil . . . [*With remorse*] No, I shouldn't have driven them off . . . I'm still weak . . . with frayed nerves . . . from the first birth, the first death in the family . . . And I don't even know what the customs are . . . [*Deep in thought*] What did Father say about them making me laugh? They didn't possess a jot of humour . . . [*The Beings return*]

FIRST BEING: We won't leave until we make the mother of the dead one laugh.

SECOND BEING: Who is the mother of the dead one?

IRINA: Huh! It's a long time since she had anything to laugh with . . .

THIRD BEING: We'll put her teeth in.

IRINA: It's not only a question of teeth . . .

FIRST BEING: And the nashers?

IRINA [*laughing*]: Not only a question of back teeth . . .

SECOND BEING [*mimicking fear*]: Has her hair fallen out?

IRINA [*amused*]: Very likely . . .

FIRST AND THIRD BEINGS [*prancing about*]: She's laughed! She's laughed!

SECOND BEING: You are the dead one's mother.

IRINA: Sorry: his daughter . . .

FIRST BEING: Excuse us: his mother . . .

THIRD BEING: We knew you from your laugh.

IRINA: That's enough, good people, you've made my head whirl . . . Thank you for the vigil . . . Now I'll manage alone . . . and then my husband and the people will surely be here soon . . . Is it still raining outside?

FIRST BEING [*to the others*]: Get up and go.

SECOND BEING: Giddie-up! and go did you say? [*Laughs*]

FIRST BEING: Get up and go, I said.

IRINA: Go on, get out! Disappear! Make yourselves scarce! Go to hell! Go and take a long walk on a short plank! [*Laughs*] Look how expressive our language is. I'm sorry if . . . [*With all her energy*] Get out!

FIRST BEING: All right, we'll go. Don't keep on at us. We'll go.

IRINA: Get the hell out of here! Go on! Clear off! Bugger off!

SECOND BEING [*angrily*]: Don't shout at us, you shrew! Why have you shot your mouth off?

THIRD BEING [*to the second*]: Why get angry? [*Pointing to Irina*] She's a woman. The head's a goose and the body's a fox. [*Laughs*]

FIRST BEING: Anyway, we've done our duty ten times over. We've predicted, we've vigilled, we've tempted and bedevilled. We've brought the water from the viper. Long we sought her, no more water. Fetch the besoms, ride away, in the saddle, we've had our say! [*They exit*]

IRINA [*Left alone, she doesn't know what to do. She reswaddles the baby. Picks it up. Goes over to the dead one, arranges the winding sheet, etc. Then she goes to the window and leans her cheek against it.*]: It wasn't right for me to loose my temper like that. But those people seemed to be doing it on purpose. Making me lose my temper, talk nonsense and offend them. Outside it's pitch black. [*Looking about her*] But here it's . . . good . . . Anyway a quiet little corner . . . that is, we've nothing to get upset about. [*Catches sight of the coffin*] There is something to get upset about . . . But you mustn't mourn . . . because, when all's said and done, life is beautiful. [*laughs freely*] When all's said and done, life is beautiful. [*A strange noise is heard in the room*] I thought I heard a tinkling . . . [*Listens*] . . . so pure . . . [*Listens again*] . . . a swirling . . . [*In a corner from under the floor a spring of water gushes*] Look at that! [*A spring swirling in the house*] What a wonder! Could it be a good omen? Yes a good omen. Springs always predict abundance, a cornucopia of abundance just like a woman. You've seen in paintings: a woman with a pitcher aslant her arms, from which the water trickles and the whole painting is called 'The Spring'. And look at me now, a cornucopea, only there's no way I can take this spring to my arms. When I was little I used to discover springs in the dales and when I unblocked them, they suddenly began singing. [*In another corner, another spring gushes out more violently*] There! It's as if those little rivulets from long ago had come now to thank me, right here on the spot. But what can I hear next door? [*She rushes into the dead man's room*] It's decided to rise from under the bed. Yes, yes . . . springs are a good sign . . . of plenty. This year we've escaped a drought. Look, the water gushes . . . from the earth, from the floor, from the cellar . . . [*Somewhat afraid*] That means the cellar's flooded and then . . . What on earth? Are we living on a layer of water? [*Several streams eddy. Then outside one can clearly hear the torrent of swirling water.*] It's rained so much . . . that the earth can't take another drop . . . Apart from that, the underground springs have come to life . . . What a good idea the dam was . . . It must be strengthened by any means. That's all we'd need – the dam to break and the river to set off through the houses . . . We can cope with the local water . . . barricade it off one way or another . . . [*Takes pots, pans and buckets to fill them*] That's the problem. Everything happens at once . . . but anyway I must face up to things . . . I've got responsibilities. [*Points to the cradle and then to the coffin*] . . . to society . . . to myself . . . I'm a mother. [*The water has filled part of the room to the depth of a hand*] Don't worry, I'll manage. [*Shouts at the springs*] Out . . . Get out! . . . [*Gives a deep sigh*]

CURTAIN

Act 2 Scene 1

Three days have passed.
The water has covered everything. Many houses have been swept
down the hill. The teacher's house is still standing, but the roof has
been carried away by the storm. The rooms are seen as in a trans-
parent aquarium. Everything that can float – boxes, bottles, the
bucket, etc. – all float, as here too the water level is very high, almost
up to the mattresses, and it is still rising. In some places one can see
small whirlpools. IRINA, *in bed, with the baby carefully swaddled to*
keep it dry, for that would be the last straw. On the other bed – the
coffin. After the curtain has gone up – a long pause to allow the full
extent of the disaster to be measured. During this pause, Irina sneezes
a number of times. After each sneeze she says "Bless you".

IRINA: The situation's not desperate. It's not by any means . . . as
   desperate . . . as one might think . . . as appearances might lead
   you to believe . . . certain appearances . . . [*To the child wrapped*
   up on the bed] Don't cry, my love . . . Let's not panic . . . you've
   nothing to fear . . . [*Crying*] Why should you cry and not me? . . .
   Because you couldn't care less . . . You arrived with your bag on
   your back . . . as they say . . . you didn't work, you didn't sweat
   . . . to feel sorry . . . We struggled . . . for this house . . . which is
   now no more . . . well it is, but see [*Points upwards*] . . . the sky,
   and not through a window . . . Anyway, a mother's duty is to
   introduce you to our belongings . . . and from now on they're
   your belongings too . . . Look how they swim! [*She plunges her*
   hand into the water and fishes out a slipper or something] [*With*
   pride] Here is your father's house . . . You'll remember it for the
   rest of your life, because it's the house where you were born . . .
   It's solid, very solid . . . since it withstood the shocks of giving
   birth . . . Of course you've no idea how children are made . . . It's

79

hard, bloody hard . . . In fact they're easy to make, but difficult to deliver . . . Anyway, it's good to have a little corner of our own, to get away from it all. It's nice and warm in your little bed . . . like in grandfather's bed . . . That one sleeping over there . . . is Grandfather, that's what he's called . . . see? . . . [*Pointing to the coffin*] . . . He's got a little house . . . He left us the big one . . . He's made himself a small, small, small, quiet house . . . because he wants to retire . . . to the countryside . . . where birds sing . . . and grass grows . . . That's his weakness . . . to hear birds sing and grass grow . . . through his hair . . . in fact it was his sickness . . . You know, after two thousand years bones begin to bud . . . it's very odd! . . . You see green bones . . . Maybe all the forests are nothing but huge boneyards which have a few millenia on their backs. What am I talking to you about millenia for, when you're only three days old? [*Laughs*] So . . . all round us are our belongings . . . Now don't ask me where the cattle are! Like a true peasant's son . . . that is who's born in the countryside . . . the first thing you'd be asking me is where are the cattle. [*Sadly*] They have been but are no more . . . the water has taken them . . . and carried them downstream . . . So – no more cattle. Why hide the fact? . . . No more poultry. The hens were the first to pay toll to the deluge, poor things, and finally the turkeys . . . the geese and ducks still float . . . but for how long? Everything's gone . . . lock, stock and barrel. Never mind, Mummy will buy you some . . . plastic ones, so you'll know what they looked like . . . Don't worry . . . plastic imitations are very good . . . quite perfect . . . The situation's not desperate . . . And our neighbours are no better off either . . . [*Listens*] Until a short time ago you could hear great wails, cries . . . shouts for help . . . But now . . . [*Listens carefully*] nothing . . . They've quietened down . . . whether they got help or not. In any case it's quiet . . . The flood's only local . . . here . . . because, let me tell you all about this water . . . This water, my boy . . . is rain water . . . What am I talking about? It's flood water! Believe me, I lived to see the deluge . . . and you lived as well . . . I mean you were born to see it . . . now – the waters will go down, the Tower of Babel . . . and all the rest . . . I'm joking . . . I'm that sort of person . . . Every-thing will be all right . . . better and better. We'll recover before you can say 'fish' – there's a fish! [*Child cries*] Don't cry . . . the neighbours will hear you . . . the ones whose earth shakes beneath their feet . . . Why upset them even more? If we can't even lend them a hand . . . You can be thankful we're still alive . . . Are we alive? Of course we are. Look around at how life swarms! . . . We live well . . . for better or for worse, we live well . . .

CURTAIN

Act 2 Scene 2

In a moment of stillness shouting can be heard from somewhere outside.

THE VOICE: Anyone left in there? Heh! Is there anyone still living in that house? [*Calling out loudly.*] He-e-eh!
IRINA: I think I can hear someone . . . or am I starting to imagine things?
THE VOICE: Yoo-oo-oo!
IRINA: Yes . . . yes . . . I think it's a man. [*Calling.*] Who is it?
THE VOICE: I think I heard someone. [*Calling.*] It's me.
IRINA: Who are you?
THE VOICE: My name's Titu . . .
IRINA: Titu? Titu, what?
THE VOICE: Joker . . .
IRINA: The baby's crying, I can't hear you so well . . .
THE VOICE: Joker.
IRINA: Joker! [*Laughs.*] . . . Are you Alexandru Joker's boy? Come here . . . 'cos it's the end of the world.
THE VOICE: I can't. I'm in a tree.
IRINA: What are you doing there?

THE VOICE: Sitting.

IRINA: Sitting?

THE VOICE: Sitting talking . . .

IRINA: . . . to the water . . .

THE VOICE: With my fiancée . . . 'cos we just got engaged . . . The parents were against it . . . but we chose the right moment . . . Lucky we both climbed this ashtree . . .

IRINA: Well done . . . and who is the girl?

THE VOICE: Waterman's daughter. If the worst comes to the worst . . . tell them we got engaged . . . so everyone will know . . . But who are you? . . . Aren't you that young schoolma'am?

IRINA: Yes.

THE VOICE: I thought it was your house . . . It was the only one left . . . all round you is water . . . and my ash tree . . . If you climbed on the roof . . . It's just like being at the sea . . . Have you been to the sea?

IRINA: Not yet . . .

THE VOICE: Me neither . . . [*Pause.*]

IRINA: How long have you been up there?

THE VOICE: Well . . . one, two . . . This must be the third day . . .

IRINA [*afraid*]: What? Has it been that long? . . . It seemed just a moment ago . . .

THE VOICE: You didn't realize 'cos you were sheltered . . . But up here . . . We saw it all . . . It was like the end of the world . . . so many things swept away . . . Whole houses – Can you imagine?

IRINA: But the people . . . Did they get away? . . .

THE VOICE: Some of them did . . . but for those caught out, at the start, unprepared . . . when the dam broke . . . so much stuff wasted. They've made human chains . . . but they can't get into the marshes . . . They're up on the hill . . . watching . . . because some of the boats have been going round and round like this . . .

IRINA [*afraid*]: Oh, Good God! Did anything happen?

THE VOICE: What should happen?

IRINA: I've been waiting for someone with a boat . . . my husband . . .

THE VOICE: What . . . hasn't he come back yet?

IRINA: No . . .

THE VOICE: He saved lots of people . . . especially children . . . about fifteen of them . . . He came all the way from the next village . . . when he heard about it . . . with his boat pulling against the current . . . It was almost a miracle . . . 'cos if you were up here you'd see how fast the water's flowing . . . and by boat it's as if you're climbing up Niagara . . . I've not been to Niagara either, but I heard about it . . .

IRINA [*breathlessly*]: Is he alive? Tell me . . .

THE VOICE: Well . . . he was . . . that's all I know . . . He was somewhere around here in his boat . . . But from here you can't see so well . . . Now, if you were to climb up on the roof . . .

IRINA: I can't move a step . . .

THE VOICE: Then stay still then . . . He'll come . . . He must be coming . . . I'm waiting for him to . . . 'Cos he was a sailor . . . It's only them now . . . and the army . . . that's lucky . . . Even some in helicopters flew over us here . . . You mustn't think folk have deserted you . . . that some have taken shelter . . . and forgotten about others . . .

IRINA: They couldn't see me from the helicopter, but why didn't they get you?

THE VOICE: They took others . . . Just when they were coming for us, we happened to be near one of them high voltage pylons . . . 'cos we clung on to that at first . . . but then we kept slipping down . . . and slipping down . . . and in the end fell . . . We only just managed to hang on to this ash tree . . . Though how long that'll stay standing I don't know . . . And the helicopters can't get low enough' cos of the cables . . .

IRINA: Are you all right there?

THE VOICE: Same as in any tree . . . but better . . . than on the pylon . . . ohh, while we were on that it was terrible . . . and we kept slipping down like this . . . and only when our soles touched the water . . . we quickly hauled ourselves up again . . . 'cos fear gave us strength . . . When we saw all of them drowned . . . Can you tell if the electricity has been turned off yet?

IRINA: I think so . . . our radio doesn't work anymore . . . But why do you want to know? Why are you the only one talking? [*In a different tone, more encouragingly*] Hey, girl, aren't you going to say anything? That fiancé of yours is doing all the talking . . . [*In a friendly manner*] Go on, let her get a word in! [*Cooing*] If you knew what a wonder I've got in this cradle . . . Aren't you coming to see him? He'd be glad to see some proper people instead of masked Fates, or people pretending to be ghosts . . . That is . . . you'd probably like to come . . . but how do you get across the water? . . . Look I'm talking nonsense . . . [*Sighs*] What on earth made you tie yourself to a man . . . for life . . . just at a watershed [*Pause*] On the other hand, you did right . . . So what! If you

always chose the moment, you'd never do anything in life. Look, I
gave birth just when the dam was about to break . . . [*Laughs,
then is afraid*] and when Father was dying. We'll never be able to
part life from death . . .

THE VOICE [*shyly*]: And the wonder, is he alive?

IRINA [*laughing*]: I should say! Of course he's alive . . . He cries . . .
One minute he wants the breast, the next he wets himself . . . He
has no idea where he is, and that one extra drop . . . whatever it
might be . . . could be the very drop to overflow the glass . . . I
mean . . . it could carry the house away . . .

*The child begins to cry. Irina tends to it for a few moments. The voice
is heard outside humming a melody.*

IRINA [*after a time*]: What are you doing? Singing?

THE VOICE: Yes, but I haven't got much of a voice . . .

IRINA [*not knowing what to say*]: Anyway . . . a human voice . . .
Look, now I'm not frightened of death anymore, 'cos there's more
of us . . . Do you know what I was thinking?

THE VOICE: What?

IRINA: Well, don't get angry if you think it's stupid . . . Maybe you
have someone already . . .

THE VOICE: I don't understand. Have who?

IRINA: Sponsors – witnesses . . . Maybe you've already got witnesses.
'Cos if you haven't, I was thinking that I'd like to be one . . . I
mean us, me and my husband, when he comes . . . and when the
water's gone down, gone back to its source . . . Well, what do you
think? [*Silence*] I see, I shouldn't have suggested it, I've upset
you . . .

THE VOICE: No, you haven't. Why? Yesterday we had need of a
witness, everything would've been all right . . . yesterday, when
she was still alive . . .

IRINA [*afraid*]: Who was still . . .

THE VOICE: She . . . the bride . . . I mean . . .

IRINA [*understanding*]: Ah! My God!

THE VOICE: I don't even know how it happened . . . Could she have
caught cold? I was frightened she'd loose her mind . . . You
know . . . when you find yourself like this . . . but not she . . . she
was very brave. She even encouraged me . . . She even found the

strength to tell me . . . we'd reached the end of our – tree . . . We gave each other courage. [*In a different tone*] Have you got a candle?

IRINA: I did have . . . until a short time ago they kept floating round the coffin . . .

THE VOICE: Good job you thought in advance about a coffin . . .

IRINA [*houseproud*]: It just happened like that. We're not all that good housekeepers.

THE VOICE: But you said that . . . he was alive . . . [*Afraid*] Or have you lost your mind as well? . . . Wouldn't it be funny if I'd been talking for two hours to a woman who was mad, and I'd not even noticed she was off her rocker? . . . No, I heard the child cry . . .

IRINA [*reproachfully*]: See? The coffin was for my father . . . He was getting ready to die . . . He was near to death, but didn't know the moment it would happen . . .

THE VOICE: Not a good one . . .

IRINA: Not a good one, but he died all the same and of a natural death. That was a kind of revenge . . . I mean when everyone's landing in hot water, rushing and dying suddenly and tragically, to die naturally . . . and to have a coffin . . . on your doorstep, prepared in time . . . Anyway, everything beautifully planned, in good time . . .

THE VOICE: Ah, that's why . . . you were talking about the candles . . .

IRINA: But . . . why do you still need them?

THE VOICE: You're right . . . Now she's cold . . . But any rate . . . [*Groans*] Ohhh, my hand's gone numb. I've been holding onto her with one hand ever since she couldn't hold on for herself . . . I could feel her slowly getting colder and colder . . . I'm so glad we managed to get engaged . . . At least we had some joy in this life, however small . . . 'cos that's an important step . . . Ahhh, but how numb my arm's gone . . .

IRINA: You've got to be strong . . . Tell yourself you've got to live so that . . . so that you can tell them . . . Now you've another responsibility . . . to her . . . You mustn't be afraid . . . Best sing something . . .

THE VOICE: What shall I sing?

IRINA: I don't know . . . anything you like . . . a song . . .

THE VOICE: [*Pause*] I can't think of anything, just like that . . .

IRINA: Then I'll sing . . . Do you mind a lullaby? I'll be able to get the baby to sleep at the same time . . .

THE VOICE: My sleep's gone anyway . . . Sing what you like . . . a lullaby if you want to . . .

IRINA: [*Singing in a rather forced voice*]

> Rock-a-bye baby,
> Mama's little baby,
> Grow strong and sturdy,
> Big and mighty
> As the sea, the sea.

[*She stops as if trying to find the words*] I know your mother . . . Do you think she used to sing that song to you?

THE VOICE: That's the song from where we come from . . . Me . . . I remember . . . I slept in a wash tub . . . now, well . . . different conditions, the children have a cradle . . . all sorts of toys . . . I used to play with a horseshoe . . . 'cos they were hard times . . . after the war, the drought . . .

IRINA: I was the same . . . someone made me an aeroplane from wood . . . some twigs tied with string.

THE VOICE: Shh! I think I can hear something . . . They're coming in the helicopter . . .

IRINA: I think I can hear it too —a fluttering.

THE VOICE: Helicopters don't flutter.

IRINA: You're right . . .

THE VOICE: . . . except with one wing . . . they flutter.

IRINA: You're laughing at me . . . But I did think I heard some fluttering . . .

THE VOICE: Some crows . . . or ravens . . . went past.

IRINA: Are you superstitious?

THE VOICE: No, why do you ask?

IRINA: It's just . . . that . . . I'd started to get lonely, here on my own, with a dead body floating near me, the coffin I mean . . .

THE VOICE: As far as the dead ones go, we're in the same boat!

IRINA: Can you still feel your arm?

THE VOICE: I think so . . . [*Sadly*] No . . . I can't anymore . . .

IRINA: But how can you keep holding your fiancée? Or did you let her go?

THE VOICE: No, 'cos if I let her go I would have jumped in after her . . . I'm not allowed to let her go . . . I've tied her to me with my belt . . . You know . . . even so, she's beautiful . . . As if she was sleeping. I keep expecting her to wake up any minute . . .

IRINA: You started young with life's problems . . .

THE VOICE: What do you think? Are they going to come in the next twenty-four hours? 'Cos I don't know how much longer I can hold out . . . I'll try, but . . .

IRINA: I'm sure . . . Less than twenty-four hours . . . Now, in an hour or two . . . They can't be long . . . They're bound to come. Good job you're up there in full view . . . They can see you a long way off . . . Don't forget to tell them about me . . . and to come and search the place thoroughly . . . if they come . . .

THE VOICE: As if I was on a ship . . . right at the top . . . in the crow's nest . . . But nothing can be seen on the horizon . . .

IRINA [*encouraging him*]: Don't you worry . . . The whole village is in danger . . . the alarm was raised . . . they mobilized all the forces . . . you know . . . up until a short time ago the set was on . . . all sorts of measures were announced . . . I'm really lucky to have you up there . . .

THE VOICE: Cuckoo? Cuckoo.

IRINA: What?

THE VOICE: I've remembered a song. I'm singing it . . . Cuckoo, [*Laughs*] Cuckoo.

IRINA: "The cuckoo sang for everyone, but for me, only the raven . . . "

THE VOICE: What's that?

IRINA: It's another song . . . I didn't hear the cuckoo this year . . . I don't know why . . .

THE VOICE: Well, you can hear it now . . .

IRINA: Please be a good cuckoo to me, do you hear me you "Cuckoo ash-grey bird".

THE VOICE: Cuckoo, cuckoo . . . cuckoo, cuckoo . . . [*Louder and louder*] Cuckoo, cuckoo, cuckoo, cuckoo, cuckoooo . . .

IRINA [*laughing*]: That's enough now. Stop, you're making me deaf.

THE VOICE: Cuckoo, cuckoo, cuckoo . . .

IRINA: And the water, is it rising or going down? Here in the room it seems to keep rising. I was just thinking that you probably realised the general situation . . . Maybe with God's help it'll go down . . . eh?

THE VOICE: Cuckoo . . . Cuckoo, cuckoo . . .

IRINA: He wants to scare me as well . . . [*Loudly*] Hey, you can't frighten me just like that . . . Many people have tried . . . Better make sure you don't fall off that branch . . . Tie yourself on well

87

with the belt ... And when you see the people ... coming ...
wave to them with your hand ... with your wing ... Cuckoo.
[*Starts to cry. In between sobs*] Cuckoo, you ash-grey bird.

CURTAIN

Act 2 Scene 3

IRINA *on the top of her bed, trying to turn on the radio on the wall.*

IRINA: Let's see where we stand ... [*Keeps turning the knob, but the
radio doesn't work*] Broadly speaking, we stand in bed ... but I'd
be interested in the details and perspective ... And, to be honest,
I'd welcome any kind of news ... 'cos it can't be worse than it is!
And after all, you can't live like that under the earth ... under
water ... [*Curiously*] I wonder what's new on the moon?
[*Irritated with the radio*] Say something, numbskull! [*A crackling
noise is heard*] That's it. Come in – talk ... [*More crackling
noises, then the radio is silent*] Well at any rate one can say I made
contact with the rest of the world ... I've re-established links with
the world ... The world is crackling ... and sending me
encouragement. That's what I gleaned from these crackles ...
Hold on! Soon someone from the sky ... will appear ... climbing down the rope ... from the helicopter ... He'll say: "Come
here, we've come to take you in the lobster pen." [*More crackling
noises on the radio. Irina stops fiddling with it. She stays on the
bed and studies the whirlpools in the room*] It's strange how in my
room the water swirls from right to left and in the dead one's
room from left to right ... Anticlockwise ... in my room ...
Now what does that mean? Why does the water turn time back

88

for me? You can't hear the rain now . . . [*Listens*] It hasn't been
raining for sometime, and I think we are in for a drought.
[*Laughs*] Just now I dozed off for a moment and dreamt about a
corner of the Sahara . . . I think the driest corner. I was playing in
the sand . . . making sand-timers from dead camels . . . I don't
know how it worked . . . I was pouring sand into their ears . . .
and it flowed out through their hooves . . . and eventually the
camels overturned . . . and I found myself pouring it through the
hooves . . . I also saw a fire, some hot . . . ovens . . . and at the end
me again pouring sand down the camels' throats . . . Suddenly
they erupted – volcanoes . . . You see, the camels were some
volcanoes in disguise and lava flowed to the right and to the
left . . . Luckily, I woke up . . . Only God knows . . . the meaning
of such a dream. I once saw some people who died in a fire. A
lorry overturned and caught them underneath . . . then the engine
exploded – you couldn't get close – you could see them burning
. . . and not even they could believe that suddenly, like that, out of
the blue . . . I much prefer a flood . . . and, after all, things like
that don't happen here any more . . . You mustn't loose your
head . . . have faith . . . [*To the child*] Do you hear, scamp? In a
way, I'm glad that . . . you weren't born on eiderdown.

*The water has risen even more. As the dead man's bed is lower, the
coffin starts to float.*

[*To the baby*] You've wet yourself, I don't know . . . Let's change
you. [*She changes him*] Look, Grandfather has set off . . . He's
taking his walk . . . He always went for a walk about this time.
He's got wet as well, but I'm not going to change him anymore.
Why? he's no nappies left . . . all gone! His time's run out. Just
look, what a boat! It's lucky we've got a boat in the house. Our
bed's a little higher . . . [*Gets hold of the coffin and ties it with a
sheet to her bed*] . . . Now I've got both of you close . . . close
relatives. I don't understand why the water's still rising . . .
clouded . . . [*Talking to the torrent*] Hey! I can see you're not
going to stop! Do you really intend to rise right over us in bed? It's
gone beyond a joke. [*In a different tone*] I was saying, "Beyond a
joke," when in fact it's a tragedy . . . [*Afraid anyway*] Yes, the
water really is getting into the bed . . . Better to have dreamt a

89

dream like this: Great waters . . . come to your bed . . . come one evening, great waters . . . instead of a man . . . to your bed . . . Then it would have been clear: Bad luck. If you dream of cloudy waters, it means bad luck . . . [*In the meantime she has lifted the child in her arms*] But such bad luck . . . without it being foreseen in a dream. [*Feels the water touching the soles of her feet. Takes in a breath*] It's bitten my soles . . . the wild beast . . . There! Who would have believed it. But never mind. Under exceptional situations the body becomes more resistant. The body's resistance grows in geometrical proportion while the danger rises in arithmetical progression . . . See, I've even made up a theorem . . . Unless it's the other way round . . . [*Pulls the coffin onto the flooded bed, sets the child in it*] The solution has already been found, despite the enemies . . . I didn't realize why father insisted so much on an oak coffin . . . it's as if he knew something . . . A real ark . . . If the worst comes to the worst, we'll all climb into it . . . Look, the dead one has come into bud . . . His bones have become green and have come into bud as if he had been floating for thousands of years. They can make good quality coffins if they really want to. They don't fall apart or anything . . . The ones inside come alive sooner than the oak'll rot. I don't know what's the matter with me, I tire easily . . . for the last three days I've been fighting back dark thoughts . . . and I've got tired . . . Lucky I don't sweat, the flood would have risen even more . . . [*Laughs*] No great loss without small gain. I've been wanting a herbal bath for a long time . . . Herbal baths are recommended both for nerves and regaining strength . . . There can hardly be more plants than in this tub of a flood . . . so that . . . if it were only a little warmer . . . Anyway . . . a strange feeling . . . such a strange feeling . . . when the water seizes you . . . slowly, slowly . . . As if someone was walling me up . . . beginning at my soles . . . into a large wall . . . What sort of wall, Lord . . . What sort of wall? I'd have been better staying at the dam – they could have walled me up there . . . but you see, they took pity on the child . . . and that's why the wall collapsed . . . It's my fault for not staying . . . Why did they take pity on me? They shouldn't have done, you mustn't be mean with sacrifices. You must go right to the end . . . and with serenity . . . [*Pause. Then cheerfully, as if playing hide and seek*] Here I was. [*After a pause*] That's a nice pool I'm in, look at it . . . [*Didactically*] A woman, twenty three years old . . . has rather exhausted life . . . She has shown the full measure of her abilities . . . Everything that follows tends to repeat itself . . . Even if you had children . . . a few little children, you've closed your account with life as honestly as you can . . . You came, you saw, you gave birth. You preened in the mirror . . . The women, the poets, until they reach twenty, hey, hey, they have enough time to assert themselves . . . to show the full measure of their genius . . . I am twenty-three . . . I've long passed the threshold. I shouldn't feel sorry for myself . . . I'm talking as if I were on my last legs, God forgive me. Why all this pessimism? I must stop. Not until the very last moment does man want to admit that this is really death. And is careful until the very last second . . . And now I feel like praying, just like this: "Wash the glass free from germs in which you pour poison for me . . . " At the theatre I could never stand an extreme situation. You place a character in imminent danger, and after that you cling like a leech to disaster. You inflate it, you pump it up . . . you know, you keep developing and hurrying on the imminent danger. Someone rightly said that such dramatic limits exist only in some absurd heads. Life is much more complex . . . Look, here for example . . . [*Afraid of the water*] Oooogh! This water is developing absurdly . . . But I don't find myself in an extreme situation . . . that's all the difference . . . which is essential . . . I'm sure that the one in the tree . . . who was saying cuckoo . . . [*Listens*] The poor man doesn't even say cuckoo anymore . . . if he could have managed to put down on paper what he'd seen, he would have presented the problem quite differently. Grandly . . . with the accent on the greatness of man . . . When man is truly in danger . . . how sublime he is then.

The voice is heard from outside.

THE VOICE: Cuckoo, cuckoo, cuckoo . . .

IRINA [*gladly*]: Talk of the devil . . . and there he is singing. Hey, young man . . . I was just thinking about you. Have you recovered? You felt weak, like that, but it's gone now . . . I've also felt sick a few times . . . but I couldn't give in . . . You know, I've respon-sibilities . . . I've brought a child into the world, I have to look after it. I can't afford to lose my mind . . . That's why I've been talking all the time . . . You heard me, because I talked loud enough . . . for you as well, so you don't feel lonely in your madness . . . I've never done so much compressed thinking as now . . . about certain things. They seemed to me very clear and I

91

solved them . . . theoretically . . . I was saying that I liked that idea of yours . . . to present everything hour by hour . . .

THE VOICE: Cuckoo . . .

IRINA: You seem to be singing better now . . . you're near perfection . . . or are you really a bird? Anyway, the main thing is that you're listening. That I've got someone to talk to . . . Because I've noticed the water keeps rising and I can't swim . . . and . . . I feel I've got to talk all the time . . . I don't know why . . . I remembered two lovers who had put the coffee on. It boiled over and put out the flames . . . The gas continued to leak, but they didn't notice because they were making love . . . They were in love . . . Someone had locked them in that unfamiliar little room . . . and when they realized that . . . it was too late . . . 'cos gas paralyzes you in a certain way . . . and you can see you're dying, you're conscious, but you can't move . . . you're just so amazed . . . amazed . . . When they found them, their faces were so distorted, that they had to inject them to relax the skin on their cheeks, so as not to bury them like that – in amazement. So that . . . I can't think what I was going to say . . . I keep loosing track . . . Ah! Try and smile, don't stay so tense, 'cos that's the source of all our troubles . . . we're too tense . . . Can you hear me? [*Listens*] I don't think it could have been the boy. He must have fallen off a long time ago . . . Either it just seemed so to me, or it was a real cuckoo . . . 'cos what do they care? They lay their eggs in other birds' nests . . . and come carousing to me, to me who's up to my eyes in work. [*Realizing how much the water is now covering her*] Not quite up to my eyes, but it won't be long now . . . Only my boy laughs . . . Look how he laughs . . . Good for you, learn to laugh early. In life you'll bump into many good jokes . . . Now, tell me, why were you laughing? [*Worried*] Have you gone and wet Grandfather? When babies have done something they laugh themselves silly . . . Poor Father, he should be protected, at least from above . . . Otherwise, a mess underneath, a mess all around . . . Anyway, you're on top of the situation . . . Father, long live your throne, God forgive me, 'cos it's so useful. I'll never forget this for the rest of my life . . . for the rest of my days . . . But how many are the rest of my days? Who knows when one's time comes? I feel a dizziness coming over me . . . a tiredness as boundless as this sea . . . an immense weariness. [*Divided into syllables*] Bound-less-weari-ness . . . How strange it sounds . . . Especially separated into syllables . . . Bound-less-weari-ness . . . At the end

92

all education's good for, is to separate death into syllables . . .
[*Gravely*] . . . Before the water reaches my breast . . . I'll feed him
once more . . . a good idea, at last. You keep on philosophizing
and forget to feed the baby . . . [*She opens her blouse, takes the
child from the coffin and puts him to the breast*] The breast, my
love. What is it? [*Laughing*] How should I know? A breast. I can
feel you're beginning to enjoy it already, you little rogue. What a
womanizer you'll be. Just like your father . . . Who knows what
he's up to now, since he hasn't come home . . . chasing some skirt
I dare say . . . [*Through the hole in the roof – a moonbeam
appears*] Look, the sky has cleared. One can see the stars above
like a painting where the oil has started to peel . . . They come to
mirror themselves in the lake. They're coming such a long way
just to mirror themselves in this sewer. Look, there's the breast,
and there's the cosmos. [*Watching the child suckle*] Not even the
cosmos has been properly understood, to say nothing of the
breast! It's not good for you to know everything so soon . . . It's
me who should know everything *by now* . . . There comes a
moment when you must know everything there is to know . . .
because you leave . . . and it's better to go . . . knowledgeable
. . . knowing . . . full of knowledge and . . . pale . . . [*Pause*] That
star seems to have appeared specially to give me a halo as
well . . . My small hazy halo . . . Because I've brought someone
into the world . . . [*Beginning a song*] I wear my halo like a hole in
the ice, full of those who drowned in God. [*Looking at the
suckling child*] Take your fill, boy . . . At least once, so you can
remember the milk that you sucked, when life's at its worst . . .
This is what I remembered just now . . . while my hair was turning
white . . . indeed it has turned white . . . [*Putting her hand
through her hair*] My hair tired first. Now I have the hair of a
ghost. Suddenly it's not heavy any more. In my time my hair had
gold in it . . . it fell heavy on my shoulders. And if you tested it
with your teeth, you could tell it was pure gold . . . [*Cries*] I was,
just for a moment, one of the great riches of this country. [*Pulling
herself together*] Ah! And that taste of milk . . . What I learned
there *inside*, is that all things are linked. And suddenly I found
myself torn, dislodged, thrown out of that world. [*Afraid*] I was
born! [*Face brightening up*] In that immense, nameless falling I
suddenly felt on my lips my mother's breast . . . A well of milk . . .
[*To the child*] What do you say to that? There's still milk and

honey flowing in this world. [*Hiding her breast in her blouse*] That hurt it was so full . . . It's not quite as full now . . . [*Looking at the water which has risen even more*] So I should be able to float more easily. [*Shouting, suddenly overcome with despair*] Nooo! [*Pulls herself together, puts the child on the coffin, which has risen as well. Sweetly*] Now go to sleep. What shall I sing to you? What shall I sing? [*Trying to think of a tune – then stays lost in thought, listening to the water flowing*] The water is singing . . . instead of me . . . Now that there's more light, everything's more terrifying. Yet I can't even scream. The child would wake . . . The dead would wake . . . Better to sing . . . What shall I sing? [*Pause*]

THE VOICE: Cuckoo, cuckoo . . .

IRINA: How clearly I see everything. The water is clouded, but my mind has become clear. Cleansed in cloudy water . . . everything is all right . . . [*Listens*] No one is calling for help any more. Everyone's been saved . . . everyone's at home. It's just that some of the houses float downstream . . . with a few small exceptions. [*A thought*] I wonder if my house is floating? Could I have got as far as the Danube? Could I have passed the Black Sea? Maybe right now I'm swaying on an ocean? What ocean do all the other oceans flow into? If only my man knew where to find me . . . If only he'd come faster in his boat . . . before the Black Sea flows into the black ocean . . . [*Looking lovingly at the child*] You give birth to a child once and are proud all your life, as if at any moment you could give birth to another. Women brag a great deal, to themselves. They're full of themselves, to themselves. [*As if trying to demonstrate something*] Me now, for example . . . me . . . a nobody . . . [*The water comes up to her neck. With hands above her head she holds tight to the child on the floating coffin*] would have no reason left to believe in life. Yes, that's what it seems – no reason . . . What still holds me? The coffin. What I learned *there, inside* is that everything is linked . . . But what keeps me linked now? . . . to the house . . . to the earth? The water's coming up to my chin. I have to hold my head back to speak . . . and to see that star above. Just one star . . . Maybe the roof broke especially for me to see that same star . . . which hasn't yet set . . . but seems paler . . . because day is breaking . . . and it too will be flooded by a different, stronger light. [*Watching the star*] As long as something can still be seen on the horizon . . . A beam of a star . . . or a straw . . . there's still hope . . . And if there is a single hope, there must also exist half of that hope . . . and half of the half . . . and so on forever and forever . . . The old ones knew what they were talking about. They taught us to be optimistic to the end. Oh, how I brag! Yet I feel uneasy . . . I don't know why the water makes me uneasy . . . I only regret that I hadn't enough time to think enough about him as well . . . about my man . . . Once . . . [*Trying to remember*] Once, when I was pregnant with our child, he looked at me for a long time . . . in a certain way . . . as he'd never looked before . . . I said, why are you measuring me up and down like that, from head to toe, as if you'd never seen me before. I'm still the same woman. And he said to me, and his voice was shaking . . . Just a minute, let me try to remember his exact words . . . Ah, yes. [*In a faint voice*] The way you stand upright with soft arms on your full womb, you seem to be a ruler's wife from olden times, holding the founded church. And I can almost hear a voice from beyond the disappearance of matter: "We, Ion and Ioana, by our own means have built this holy child for the eternal remembrance of this sun, of this earth . . . " [*Pause*] It's strange I should remember that just now, when the water's reaching my lips. It's as if my bump came as high as my chin again . . . [*Serenely*] It's the great womb of the sea . . . I've done my duty – [*Smiling*] The whale has done everything. Right to the bitter end, it felt responsible for the one God had implanted in the womb. It deposited him safely on dry land . . . [*Sadly*] The land was a coffin . . . [*Crying*] [*Dryly*] It's stopped raining. This is a victory of the land. I've reached the half of half of hope. Close to the infinite . . . Beyond the monotonous and mean moaning of the water, my ear hears the splashing of an oar courageously digging deep into the waves. [*Listening*] Yes . . . I hear it lowered not into clay, not into earth, but into water . . . I'm sure of it. What if those in the boat perished as well? They'll come with the helicopter. They'll save all those left in the middle of the torrent, no one will be left to chance. Thank God the roof got broken, so they can see in from above. I can almost hear that brave man . . . a nobody . . . just like me, telling his folk how he descended from the helicopter through the roof in the flooded house . . . [*Imitating*] And when I looked, I saw a child floating above the water . . . And I was about to pull him out, when I saw that something from the depths was holding him up. And when I looked again, I realized that what was holding him . . . were the hands of his mother. Poor hands! They'd gripped the little one and hadn't let him die . . . hadn't let the waves take him . . . [*Radiant with happiness*] And do you know the child was breathing . . . [*Mounting the coffin, she takes the child and lifts him above her head. Inundated with the light of an immense happiness, just one moment before the water rises above her head*] Breathe! Come on, breathe! Breathe . . .

CURTAIN

The Matrix: Swiss production, 1975.

Appendix:

POEMS

THE TWO THIEVES

The two thieves are important
As well.
One stole a candle stick,
The other beat up an animal.
Yet they too are important.
What a great thief
Is the one in the middle,
He's stolen all our glory!
If he'd not had so much publicity,
Perhaps there'd have been some left for us,
Us crucified more awry.

HYMN

Instead of roots, trees have
Saints,
Risen from the table
To kneel beneath the earth
In prayer.

Only their haloes
Are left above,
These trees,
These flowers.

And we in turn,
Will be saints,
Praying the earth
Stays round and blessed
Always.

LEVERS

So heavy is my soul
It's as if God's hanging there to pull
Down like a boulder on the balance of a well's lever.
I am his darkness from which miracles emerge
And I am the world's precursor.

A star sets out further,
Keep away from it, don't move nearer,
Look it's creaking on my breath,
Should anything stop its path
For me it could mean death.

Out of my soul rise mountains with horizons that fall,
Like stoics on nails of the fir tree,
Sometimes a cloud will gush
From a pore that dilates too much,
But more often it's a sea of salt.

I transmit myself forever in the distance
In that thousandth appearance.
Like a long-armed lever
Life from death I can sever.

Everywhere in the world I'm spread,
Thinking it over and thinking it out,
But like a well, by the universe I'm drained
At the week's end.

FRAMES

The walls of my house are covered
In frames
In which my friends
See nothing.
They think I put them there
To annoy them.

There's one gap left
Above the bed,
And I wake with a strange
Feeling
Of being watched.

In fact, on that spot
The light plays
In spherical patterns.

But there's no bulb there,
No open eye,
No phosphorous mine.

Yet despite all this
Above the bed
Someone breathes, breathes.

Who knows what star burns
Far away,
And by the strange law of reflections
Its soul now beats
Upon my wall.

Tomorrow I must put
A frame there
As well.

VISION

They no longer exist – new children,
The same parents from the beginning of the world
Continually give birth to the same children,
Who would realize the deception
If given more time.

But they're already born with moustaches
And have only the last
Seven days to live,
In which they stay rigid
In flesh and bone
As in the suits
Of astronauts.

And people really believe
That their sons will go
On an extraordinary journey
And they bring them flowers,
Which they neither see nor smell,
Because, look, they only have one day left
Out of seven.

The moment of launching approaches,
Children, be old,
Be rigid in your flesh and bone,
We'll launch you into the earth
With such great ceremony.

Even if we never receive
A single telegram from you,
At night we'll hear in sleep
The hurtling of your bodies,
Passing through each stratum,
Until when, on the other side of the planet,
Tired and blinded by darkness
You rise
In the womb of another woman.

A woman like any other woman,
Who believes that she loves,
That the child she suckles is hers,
And who, in her turn, has buried with flowers
Many children
For birth on the other hemisphere.

LOOK . . .

Look . . . objects
Are cut in two,
On one side – the objects,
On the other – their names.

There is a vast space between them,
Space for running,
For life.

Look, you are cut in two.
On one side there's you,
On the other your name.

Don't you sometimes feel, maybe in dream,
Maybe near to dream,
That over your forehead
Other thoughts superimpose,
Over your hands
Other hands?

Someone understood you for a moment
Making your name
Pass through your body,
Painful and sonorous,
Like a bronze tongue
Through the emptiness of a bell.

PRAYER

Saints,
Let me join your ranks
At least as an extra.

You're getting old,
Perhaps you feel the pain of age
Painted on your bodies
In so many stages.

Let me carry out
The humblest jobs
In nooks and crannies.

I could for instance,
Eat the light
At the Last Supper,
And blow out your haloes
When the service is over.

And, from time to time,
At half a wall's distance,
Cup my hands to my mouth
And holler, once for the believers
And once for the unbelievers:
Hallelujah! Hallelujah!

THE RUNNER

A deserted field,
Trodden down like a road,
And here and there
A book.

At great distances,
A basic book.
Firm as a rock.

Someone is coming, panting with muscles,
Healthy as a new god,
And spits on it,
On each one in a row,
Steps on them heavenly.

He tires, he's had enough,
The field stretches ahead, deserted,
Trodden down like a road,
The runner collapses, dies,
Becomes a basic book, the last word,
A sign over which one cannot pass anymore.

Panting is heard,
From beyond a figure appears,
A runner stops, spits on the sign
And disappears over the horizon.

TRUTH COMES TO LIGHT

Truth comes to light
Extremely slowly.
Following the movement technique
Of decomposure and rotting
Oil rises to the surface,
But only after it's drowned.

THE FOUNDATION

The way you stand
Upright,
With soft arms
On your full womb,
You seem the wife
Of a ruler from ancient times
Holding their founded church.

And I can almost hear a voice
Coming from beyond
The disappearance of matter:

'We, Ion and Ioana,
By our own efforts,
Have founded this sacred
Child
For the eternal remembrance
Of this sun,
Of this earth.'

LATE

It's beginning to get late in me.
Look, it's grown dark in my right hand
And in the acacia at the front of the house.
I must put out with an eyelid
All things which stayed alight,
The slippers near the bed,
The hallstand, the paintings.
As for the rest of life's belongings,
Everything that can be seen,
Even beyond the stars,
There's no point in taking those with me,
They'll continue to burn.
And in remembrance of me
I've left word
That at least on more important feast days,
The whole universe be given to the world
As alms.